The Zen Way of Counseling

A Meditative Approach to
Working with People

First published by O Books, 2009
O Books is an imprint of John Hunt Publishing Ltd., The Bothy, Deershot Lodge, Park Lane, Ropley,
Hants, SO24 0BE, UK
office1@o-books.net
www.o-books.net

Distribution in:

UK and Europe
Orca Book Services
orders@orcabookservices.co.uk
Tel: 01202 665432 Fax: 01202 666219
Int. code (44)

USA and Canada
NBN
custserv@nbnbooks.com
Tel: 1 800 462 6420 Fax: 1 800 338 4550

Australia and New Zealand
Brumby Books
sales@brumbybooks.com.au
Tel: 61 3 9761 5535 Fax: 61 3 9761 7095

Far East (offices in Singapore, Thailand,
Hong Kong, Taiwan)
Pansing Distribution Pte Ltd
kemal@pansing.com
Tel: 65 6319 9939 Fax: 65 6462 5761

South Africa
Alternative Books
altbook@peterhyde.co.za
Tel: 021 555 4027 Fax: 021 447 1430

Text copyright Svagito Liebermeister 2008

Design: Stuart Davies

ISBN: 978 1 84694 236 5

A CIP catalogue record for this book is available
from the British Library.

www.family-constellation.net

Cover Design by Hamido Kardell. Cover painting by Meera Hashimoto (For more information on
her work visit www.meera.de) Edited by Subhuti.

Printed by Digital Book Print

The Zen Way of Counseling

A Meditative Approach to Working with People

Svagito R. Liebermeister

BOOKS

Winchester, UK
Washington, USA

CONTENTS

Acknowledgments

This book is inspired by Osho, an enlightened mystic and my spiritual master, and his vision of life. Much of my understanding is owed to his teachings and his way of helping people awaken to their own spiritual reality and to their highest consciousness. The Zen stories used in this book are originally from Japanese and Chinese sources, but I first heard them while listening to Osho's discourses on Zen. They point to a truth that lies beyond logical argumentation.

Osho's Meditation Resort in India and his growth centers around the world have become a melting pot for the merger of many styles of therapy and creativity, and a meeting place for unique teachers in various fields. I have learned from many of these teachers, and I would like to make special mention of Sagarpriya Delong, who has played a pioneering role in bringing therapy in close proximity to meditation. I have been studying and teaching her Psychic Massage and Star Sapphire energy work for more than 20 years.

Some of Sagarpriya's innovative concepts are presented in this book in a more generalized form, so that they benefit to a wider audience, including people who want to work with their own methods in a more meditative way. Sagarpriya's approach to therapy is described in her book 'The Master's Touch, Psychic Massage' (Sandvik Publishing, 1994) and in a new book that will be published shortly.

I also want to mention the Pulsation approach to therapy, developed by Aneesha Dillon; Family Constellation, developed by Bert Hellinger; Somatic Experiencing, created by Peter Levine. All of these have influenced and contributed to my way of working as a therapist and to my understanding of counseling. Naturally, some of their concepts will be interwoven in this book.

I would like to thank my wife Meera, who has found a unique

way of combining art and therapy. She has been supporting my work and inspiring people to explore meditation. With her, I keep discovering new elements of the dimension of creativity and of the world of self-development that lies beyond therapy.

I want to express my gratitude to Subhuti, who has helped me to create this book in a clear and simple way. His writing skill makes the concepts in this book easy to understand without having to digest an academic vocabulary, and he took care to keep it light and focused.

There are many other sources of inspiration, especially my students and course organizers, whose interest, trust and love have always encouraged me.

"Therapy basically is meditation and love.
Because without love and meditation there is no healing possible.
When the therapist and the patient are not two, when the therapist is not a therapist only, and when the patient is not a patient anymore, but a deep I - thou relationship arises, where the therapist is not trying to treat the person, when the patient is not looking at the therapist as separate from himself, in those rare moments therapy happens, when the therapist has forgotten his knowledge and the patient has forgotten his illness and there is a dialogue, a dialogue of two beings.
In that moment between the two healing happens.
And if it happens the therapist will know always that he functioned only as a vehicle of a divine force, of a divine healing.
He will be as much grateful for the experience as the patient.
In fact he will gain as much out of it as the patient."

Osho

Introduction

This book is about spiritual therapy, which means a kind of therapy that has the vision of meditation as its essential foundation. It is not focused on a particular technique or method, but examines the core understanding of a meditative approach and in this way offers a wider and more comprehensive perspective.

Several modern approaches to therapy refer to 'mindfulness' as an important aspect of healing, which is an indirect and rather belated recognition by western researchers and psychologists of the essential importance of meditation. 'Mindfulness' really means the ability to become watchful of one's own body and mind, which is exactly what meditation is all about.

In this book, the terms 'counseling' and 'psychotherapy' are used almost synonymously, but there is a difference: counseling is a wider term that refers to any form of helping people to solve problems and develop their potential; psychotherapy refers more to a process of treatment by a trained professional who establishes a relationship with a client with the purpose of modifying or removing existing symptoms and promoting personal growth.

The use of the word 'Zen' in the title of this book requires explanation. These days, Zen is a widely used term, often with unclear meaning and little connection to its origin. Originally, the word comes from a Sanskrit root 'dhyan' and means meditation, pointing to a state of consciousness that is beyond duality and therefore difficult to either describe or define.

Zen comes from the Buddhist tradition of meditation, where the essential teaching is transmitted from a spiritual Master to a disciple, who then becomes the next Zen Master. This lineage began with Gautam Buddha and his disciples in India, but later reached to China, where 'dhyan' became 'chan,' and when it continued to Japan it became 'Zen.'

Zen, or Zen Buddhism, has a long tradition in Japan, where many different schools of meditation exist. Zen Masters are famous for their illogical, unorthodox and sometimes shocking methods of teaching their disciples, with the intention to awaken them to spiritual enlightenment. The original purpose of Zen, if one can speak of a purpose, is to help an individual make a direct experience of his true nature, rather than remaining on the level of a student who studies religious scriptures in an intellectual way.

The word Zen is now a mainstream expression in western societies and is vaguely associated with a number of images: meditation, Japanese culture, a certain style of gardening, design, architecture, painting and poetry. We associate it with stillness, simplicity and limiting something to its essential nature while removing anything that is superfluous.

The term 'Zen' is used in this book to emphasize the connection between therapy, counseling and meditation, drawing attention to the fact that meditation is the core aspect of any therapy that wants to connect to a deeper level of self-understanding and spiritual growth.

This book is offered to all those interested in combining therapy and meditation, either for gaining more understanding themselves, or finding more clarity in their work with people. As already mentioned, the principles described in this book can be applied to any kind of therapy or counseling; they are not technique oriented.

Part One of the book examines characteristics of how the human mind functions, including differences between personality and individuality, and gives a general outline of how personal transformation occurs. This includes relationship dynamics between men and women.

Part Two establishes principles of how to conduct a counseling session using the understanding introduced in Part One.

In Part Three, different approaches to therapy are compared as a way of understanding how one can look at personal issues from different angles and with a different focus. No standpoint is 'right' or 'wrong;' each approach can enrich one's vision of how human beings function and grow.

Most of the practical examples come from the author's experience in working with people in sessions, courses and training groups. The terms 'therapist' and 'facilitator' are used interchangeably, and the word 'he' denotes both genders.

~

Part One

The Essential Elements of Counseling

The first section of this book presents a basic understanding that needs to be considered by anyone who approaches therapy from a meditative standpoint. It is an effort to give linguistic expression to something that is not usually talked about, but which is often included by practitioners who embrace a meditative vision when working with people.

For example, in most schools of therapy, the teaching usually focuses on methods of treating a client. The practitioner himself, his needs and his inner attitude, are hardly ever mentioned. However, such considerations should really be at the beginning of any training in therapy. Why? Because, as we shall see, 'being' is more fundamental than 'doing.'

~

Chapter One

Therapy and Meditation

It is strange that the development of psychotherapy in western countries over the past 130 years has not embraced any concept of meditation, while the long history of meditation in eastern countries like India, China and Japan contains no concept of psychotherapy. Until recently, psychotherapy and meditation have never met and it is puzzling because they both focus on the human mind and human consciousness. They are natural partners in the same quest of understanding who we are as conscious beings.

It is generally agreed that modern psychology began in Germany in 1879 when Wilhelm Wundt founded a laboratory and clinic dedicated to psychological research in Leipzig. But if we look at the wider field of psychotherapy, or psychological counseling, where one person tries to help another person gain more understanding of his own attitudes, feelings, motives and beliefs, then, of course, psychotherapy has been going on much, much longer, ever since language and communication began.

A general inquiry into the nature of the human mind, or psyche, is evident in the historical records of many ancient cultures, including Egypt and Greece, but it was not until the eighth and ninth century CE that the first mental hospitals were established. This pioneering effort was made by medieval Muslim physicians working in Cairo, Damascus and Baghdad, who were able to diagnose and treat psychological illnesses such as depression, anxiety and delusion. This placed them far ahead of their European medical colleagues, who at the time regarded mental disorders either as the work of the devil or as side-effects of physical diseases, requiring purging, bleeding, constraint, punishment or exorcism. The idea of rehabilitating mentally sick people through reasoning, moral support and encouragement came several hundred years later.

Two Schools: Freud and Behaviorism

Gradually, however, a more enlightened attitude prevailed and by the time Sigmund Freud opened his first neuropsychiatric clinic in Vienna in 1886, the treatment of mental illness as a separate category of medicine and the study of the human mind as an independent science was spreading rapidly through universities and medical schools in both Europe and the United States.

Freud's discovery of the unconscious mind through a combination of hypnosis, free association and dream interpretation created a revolution in how we perceive ourselves, introducing the disturbing idea that the motives for our actions can be hidden even from ourselves. Freud's method, called psychoanalysis, became the first major school of psychotherapy in the twentieth century.

Behaviorism, developed in the 1920s, became the second school and criticized the Freudian approach as unscientific. It confined itself to the study of observable behavior, maintaining that different forms of behavior can be described without recourse to internal events, or to a hypothetical concept like the human mind.

The division of psychotherapy into these two basic schools provoked a debate that continues today. Psychoanalysis and its founders, such as Freud, Jung and Adler, were making groundbreaking discoveries about the internal workings of the mind, but their findings, though helpful to their clients, were criticized as being too speculative and not objectively verifiable. Meanwhile, the founders of behaviorism, such as Ivan Pavlov and B.F. Skinner, were being criticized by their opponents for reducing man to a mere biological mechanism.

Subjective Reality and Science

This struggle reflects a wider issue. Ever since its origins, modern psychology has been trying to gain recognition as a science by proving the internal workings of the mind objectively. But at the core of the mind lies a subjective reality that continues to elude systematic observation and definition.

For example, when a client comes to a therapist with a psychological problem, he will be treated through a particular method or technique for a period of time, but then, at a certain point, the therapist needs to check whether the technique is working. There may be changes in observable behavior – the client may look more cheerful, more relaxed – but it is also possible that there are no external, objectively-measurable signs of change.

The most common method of checking is to ask the client, "How are you feeling?"

The client may respond, "I'm feeling much better, thank you."

This answer is subjective. It may be true, or it may not. It may simply be that the client wants to please the therapist. So the dilemma in this particular field of 'science' is that there needs to be some kind of objective standard, but this standard cannot be applied or observed in the ordinary way, because it is about a subjective reality.

The effectiveness of the treatment is measured, ultimately, by a subjective state, not by observable criteria. Of course, if the client has been suffering from a behavioral problem, such as kleptomania, and is now behaving differently – for example, he no longer goes shoplifting in local department stores – this can be said to be scientific evidence, because it can be demonstrated. But many, if not most, psychological issues are not so easily observed.

Humanistic Psychology: the Third School

Humanistic psychology, a third school of psychotherapy emerging in the 1950s, made matters even more difficult by rejecting the medical model established by the Freudians and the

Behaviorists. The new school asserted that instead of focusing exclusively on the task of helping mentally ill people become "normal," psychology should also be using "normal" as a springboard to explore further human potential.

In the 1960s, five basic principles of humanistic psychology were laid down by James Bugental and generally accepted by his colleagues:

1. Human beings cannot be reduced to components.
2. Human beings have in them a uniquely human context.
3. Human consciousness includes an awareness of oneself in the context of other people.
4. Human beings have choices.
5. Human beings are intentional, they seek meaning, value and creativity.

Founders of the new school included Abraham Maslow and Carl Rogers, who emphasized that psychology should be interested in uniquely human issues, such as the nature of self, the possibility of self-actualization, the cultivation of health, hope, love, creativity, being, becoming, individuality, and meaning — in short, the understanding of what it means to be human. In doing so, they moved psychotherapy further away from science and closer to spirituality.

In this context, the term 'psychotherapy' took on a much wider meaning. For example, in the 1970s people began to participate in therapy groups not just to cure problems like addiction or neurosis, but to explore their own hidden emotions and attitudes. Groups in places like the Esalen Institute in California became laboratories where normal social restraints were discarded so that participants could experience what lay beneath the surface of their 'civilized behavior.' Many discovered that by venting suppressed negative emotions such as anger they had more access – at least temporarily — to positive feelings like love and a state of relaxed well-being.

Therapy and Meditation: First Meeting

It was at this point, during the 1970s, that therapy and meditation met for the first time. In a general sense, it happened in Europe and America, when a wave of interest in Indian spirituality and meditation techniques spread not only through the so-called 'alternative' sub-culture but also through mainstream media and fashion trends. In centers like Esalen, primal therapy rubbed shoulders with yoga asanas and Sanskrit mantras.

In a more specific sense, psychotherapy was embraced in India itself and used as a bridge to meditation by an innovative and controversial mystic called Bhagwan Shree Rajneesh, who later became known as Osho. Osho traveled widely in India during the 1960s and early '70s, experimenting with active and cathartic meditation techniques, then in 1974 settled in Pune, where an international community grew around him.

Osho's approach was that cathartic therapies could be used to clean the mind of tension and help the physical body become more relaxed. He subscribed to the views of Wilhelm Reich, originally one of Freud's students, who asserted that suppressed emotions are locked in the physical body as muscle 'armoring' and as blocked or stagnant energy. Osho adapted this discovery for his own purposes, saying that once these tensions are released it is easier for people to sit silently in meditation.

What is Meditation?

This brings us to the question "What is meditation?" and to find the answer we need to go back 2,500 years in India to the time of Gautam Buddha.

Buddha did not invent meditation, but he gave it a clarity and methodology that made it more accessible to ordinary people. He developed the technique of Vipassana, in which the meditator sits quietly, placing his attention on his own breathing, while at the same time becoming aware of sensations in his physical body and his thinking process. Slowly, as the technique deepens, the meditator comes to realize that the faculty of awareness with which these phenomena are experienced and observed is a state of pure subjectivity. In other words, the one who is aware of the mind and the body is one who is above and beyond the mind and body.

It is an experience of consciousness in its purest state, free of attachment to both the physical body and the mind. According to Buddha, this consciousness flowers into a permanent state of enlightenment in which the meditator exists without identification with the mind and body, in a state of transcendental unity, where any sense of 'self' disappears and dissolves into a universal consciousness.

As explained in the introduction, Buddha used the Sanskrit word 'dhyana' to describe the state of consciousness that is beyond thinking, and this is what is known in Japan as 'Zen' and in English as 'meditation.'

The Mind Studying the Mind

Now, perhaps, we can see more clearly the paradox in which Western psychology finds itself. Unlike the experience of mystics like Buddha, who have the ability to perceive the mind from a state that is beyond the mind, psychology tries to understand the mind through the mind itself.

Any study of mind done by mind leads to what is known in logic and mathematics as a dialectical contradiction that cannot be easily solved. In Korea and Japan this has been called a 'Koan,' a puzzle that does not have any solution, but which is nevertheless given by Zen Masters to their disciples as a strategy to lead them beyond mind and logic.

The basic question is how one dimension can reflect back on itself. For example, there is the famous dialectic contradiction in which a librarian is ordered to make a list of all the books contained in the local library, then send one copy of it to the central library and keep one copy himself. Now the question arose for the librarian: if the book containing the list of all the other books should be regarded as a book itself, and, if so, should it be on the list? If it is not on the list, then one book has not been categorized. If it is put on the list, then one book contains itself and is therefore in an entirely separate category from all the other books.

The point is clear: ultimately, one can understand something only when one is on a separate, or higher plane. If this applies to ordinary scientific study of objectively measurable matter, it must apply even more to psychology, which necessarily includes subjective as well as objective phenomena.

What is Normal?

Another point to consider is that psychotherapy's basic intention is to bring a mentally 'sick' person back to normal functioning through an understanding and analysis of the mind. But what is considered 'normal' has been a controversy in all psychological literature and schools of psychotherapy. In fact, what one society may regard as 'normal' may be considered 'abnormal' by another society or group. There are really no objective standards for normality or sanity.

Even within the same society, messages about what is normal can be conflicting. Even in the same family, it can happen. There have been studies about double-binds, for example, by Paul Watzlawick, the Austrian-born therapist and philosopher, showing that as children we grow up in situations where we are continuously confronted with conflicting messages that in extreme cases lead to schizophrenia. Bert Hellinger's studies with family systems show that schizophrenia is the result of one child having to represent two opposing and conflicting members of a single family system.

The mind tends to become paralyzed when confronted with

opposing realities, but this is happening to us all the time, which is why Dr. Watzlawick gained widespread popularity through such books as "The Situation is Hopeless but not Serious," "Ultra-Solutions: How to Fail Most Successfully" and with a book chapter called "Insight Causes Blindness." He advocated humor, communication with others and less thinking as the best remedies for mental problems.

Duality causes stress, especially when we are asked to identify with both sides of the coin at once. But the underlying problem is that mind itself functions through duality, having been trained in most western countries to operate according to the dictates of Aristotelian logic: "If A then not B…" and so on. Mind is therefore responsible for creating its own dilemma. So the solution cannot come from the world of psychology, however sophisticated, because it is a product of mind.

No End to Therapeutic Processes

Even the greatest psychologists of our time had the same fears, problems and nightmares as their patients, sometimes even more. Freud, for example, never allowed anyone to psychoanalyze him, because he knew it would expose him, showing that he possessed the same neuroses and suppressed sexual obsessions as everyone else. Carl Gustav Jung, his most famous student, was tormented by the fear of death his whole life.

No human being has ever been completely psychoanalyzed and there seems to be no possibility of it happening. At best, people who have been in psychoanalysis for years arrive at a place of adjustment to daily life and acceptance of their own frailties, but the actual process of analyzing the mind can continue indefinitely. When one problem is solved, immediately several new ones emerge, demonstrating the mind's creative efficiency in producing things to worry about. Arthur Janov, the founder of Primal Therapy, had the idea to create an exhaustive process through which all of one's personal traumatic experience – rooted in unexpressed childhood pain — could be exposed and resolved, once and for all, but he could never demonstrate that this process had been successfully concluded in any of his clients.

Witnessing the Mind

Our curiosity about the workings of the mind in Western countries contrasts markedly with attitudes in an Eastern country like India, which has never really developed any profound psychology. Indian culture is very sophisticated and goes back thousands of years. For example, in giving birth to the language of Sanskrit it developed a highly sophisticated means of verbal and written communication which has been found to be the root of many Western languages; it has also conducted deep explorations of art, music, philosophy, meditation and spirituality, but has paid little attention to psychological processes.

How is this possible? According to Osho, who has compared Western and Eastern cultures in many of his books, Indian mystics and seers disregarded the workings of the mind because they understood that the state of enlightenment, spiritual liberation, oneness with the divine, is attained only by going beyond the mind. These mystics created many different methods for attaining higher states of consciousness, such as a wide range of meditation techniques, rituals of singing and chanting mantras, devotional prayer, yoga, fasting, asceticism and so on, but paid virtually no attention to the mind's thinking process.

In Japan, the tradition of Zen Buddhism has focused more on the mind, but only as a challenge to be transcended. Bodhidharma, the Indian mystic who was the first patriarch of Zen and who brought this quality of Buddhism from India to China, told his disciples that the best way to actualize their 'buddha nature,' was to learn the technique of 'beholding the mind.' This was a variation on Gautam Buddha's original technique of watching the sensations of both mind and body, and later became ritualized in Japan, Korea and other countries in the practice of 'Zazen.'

Osho, in his own approach, draws from these ancient techniques, but describes the same process as 'witnessing,' a way of effortlessly watching the mind without being identified with its thoughts, dreams and memories. Through this process of 'witnessing' the mind slows down, gaps appear between chains of thought, and a deeper state of inner silence or 'No Mind' is glimpsed. Simple though it may sound, this state of watchfulness is not easy to attain. Identification with the mind is one of our strongest habits as human beings, dating back millennia.

A New Form of Counseling

So the approaches developed by Western and Eastern cultures have been different, almost opposite. It is changing now, of course, as modern Western lifestyles impact countries like India and Japan, transforming ways of thinking, while spiritual approaches like Zen Buddhism and Hinduism increasingly influence Western religious ideas. There is a cross-cultural mix occurring that will hopefully benefit both sides.

A similar mix is needed in the field of psychotherapy. Up to now, therapists in Western countries have been busy examining the causes of our problems, such as early childhood conditioning and traumatic experiences from the past, while Eastern mystics offer no such analysis but rather focus on qualities like silence, presence, relaxation, being in a 'here and now' state. But there is no reason why these two approaches should not join hands and be used in harmony with each other.

An interesting by-product of Osho's synthesis of Western therapy and Eastern meditation is a new approach to counseling based on the understanding that therapy and meditation can effectively work together for the benefit of individual clients. Through therapy one can achieve a certain harmony or peacefulness within the mind, while through meditation one can dis-identify with mental preoccupation and relax into a deeper state of well-being.

The nature and practical application of this new form of counseling therapy is the subject of this book and is explained in the following chapters.

Chapter Two

Mind and Being

In recent years it has become fashionable to study the human mind through the discipline of "cognitive science," a term that was first applied in the 1970s to research into the creation of artificial intelligence, but which has been expanded to embrace the workings of the human bio-computer inside our heads.

One of the principles of this emerging science is that there are three ways in which the brain and mind can be analyzed, and these resemble the workings of an ordinary computer:

1. Physical. This is our bio-computer hardware, the mechanism of the brain.
2. Behavioral. This is our software, the psychology of the mind.
3. Function. This is the operating system that allows the software and hardware to communicate.

For example, right now you are looking at a series of symbols on this page – we call them 'letters' and 'words' – and through them you understand what I am trying to communicate to you. This is software in action. Simultaneously, as you are deciphering these symbols, neurons in your brain are firing in a certain sequence. This is hardware. The two activities are connected by a third process: function. So this is the way modern research is moving, using multiple levels of analysis to understand the brain and mind, and breakthroughs in so-called "artificial intelligence" are claimed when machines successfully replicate this method of functioning.

Modern trauma theory, which these days is regarded as one of the most advanced and fascinating areas of psychological inquiry, uses a three-layer model to understand the brain-mind phenomenon, which can be summarized as follows:

1. The Brain Stem and Reptilian Complex, also known as the 'aquatic' or 'reptilian' part of the brain. This area is instinct-oriented and includes response to pain, fear of strangers, rage, issues of fight-or-flight. It regulates processes that are essential for our survival and are not voluntarily controllable. In other words, when our survival seems to be threatened, this part of our brain will want to take over without consulting the higher, rational areas.
2. The Limbic System. This is sometimes called the 'mammalian brain' because it is similar to the brain of more primitive mammals and is the source of emotions, some aspects of personal identity, and some memory functions, including the development of long-term memory.
3. The Neo Cortex, also known as the 'primate' part of the brain. This is the thinking, or cognitive part that sits on top of the other two and has connections to both. In humans, it controls highly evolved thinking processes such as reason and speech. Here, too, we find the ability to create and comprehend culture, art and literature, and the qualities of self-reflection and self-consciousness.

In situations of stress, when an individual's survival may be in danger, the lower centers of the brain act quickly and powerfully through the autonomous nervous system to generate a large amount of energy necessary for fight or flight, without consulting the thinking part of the brain. When the threat recedes, this excess energy needs to be discharged through the body, so the organism can return to its normal functioning state, something that happens naturally in animals without difficulty or inhibition.

In humans, however, there is a problem: just as the lower brain centers can override the Neo Cortex when preparing for fight or flight, the Neo Cortex also has an ability to override impulses from lower brain centers, and in this way the discharge of excess energy is often disturbed, or inhibited. According to trauma theory, this is one of the causes of post traumatic stress, in which the individual's nervous system continues to react involuntarily as if danger is still present, while consciously he knows that it is long past. It is as if the lower centers of the brain have not yet come to know this, so they keep putting the organism on alert without finding a way to discharge the energy.

Trauma healing is a way of helping the brain's lower centers complete their impaired impulses and integrate the powerful survival energy that has become stuck or 'frozen' in the body.

Identification is the Problem

Eastern mysticism takes a more fundamental position than either cognitive science or trauma theory. From the mystical perspective, it is not just a question of understanding the relationship between various areas of the brain, and between the brain and the mind. Why not? Because mind itself is seen as the problem. Mind itself is viewed as the malaise from which we are suffering. Or, rather, it is our identification with the functioning of the mind that creates our difficulties. We are so identified with the mind, so glued to its thoughts and feelings, that we have no understanding that we can be free from it.

For example, in ordinary life, when we feel sad, we say "I am sad;" when we are angry, we say "I am angry." There is no distinction between the sense of "I" and the feeling, or mood, that is our current state of mind. Almost all human suffering is, in one way or another, connected to some form of identification. For example, at the root of national and religious wars lies the fact that two opposing groups of people are identified with different beliefs, and these beliefs are programmed into their minds.

Even small things, like identification with a football team, can trigger anger and violence. If, for example, Croatia beats England

and pushes it out of the European nations soccer competition, as happened in 2008, suddenly there is a wave of public hostility in Britain towards Croatia as a country, which was never there before.

The King and the Sufi

There is a beautiful story in the Sufi mystical tradition that illustrates the phenomenon of identification and how difficult it is for us to control it:

A king once asked a Sufi mystic to explain the nature of spiritual liberation. The mystic replied that it is a question of becoming unattached to the beliefs we have about ourselves.

The king was not impressed and laughed dismissively, "This is not great — anyone can do it."

The Sufi disagreed, saying it is really difficult, and the king challenged him to prove it.

"Very well," said the Sufi. "To prove me wrong, all you need to do is say 'I believe you' after every statement I make."

"Proceed," said the king, confidently.

"Sufism is an ancient spiritual tradition with many mysteries," began the Sufi.

"I believe you," said the king.

"We know the secrets of time."

"I believe you."

"I myself am at least four hundred years old."

"I believe you."

"I was present when you were born."

"I believe you."

"And your father was a peasant," said the Sufi

"That is a lie!" shouted the king, angrily.

"As I was saying, your Majesty," explained the Sufi. "It is truly a difficult task to drop the beliefs and ideas we have about ourselves."

We all know how difficult it is to remain calm when a love partner announces that he, or she, has fallen in love with someone else, or when we are expecting to get a promotion at work and are suddenly informed that someone else has been chosen instead.

It does not seem helpful, in such moments, to be told that the real problem is that we are identified with the beliefs, attitudes and emotions of the brain-mind mechanism, and that by dis-identifying from them we will find peace. In such moments, we would truly love to emulate the image of Gautam the Buddha, sitting in his perfect lotus position with a serene smile of detachment on his face, but when your partner of many years is about to walk out the door into the arms of someone else, such detachment seems impossible, beyond the reach of ordinary mortals like you and me.

A Process of Self-Inquiry

Instead, we may seek the help of a professional counselor, therapist, or psychologist, who is ready to listen to our problems and who may give us the feeling that he can mend what has been broken, heal whatever has been disturbing us.

In this way, we may start a process of psychological inquiry, where, in addition to trying to solve the immediate problem, we begin to look at the roots of our distress, understanding, for example, that the sense of overwhelming panic we feel at being left by a loved one originates in childhood fears of abandonment by our parents. This is the sort of help that therapy provides, in a more or less successful way, depending on the methods used and the skills of the therapist or counselor.

Even though conventional therapy is helpful at times, it is nevertheless only a small part of the real help. We often observe that, even after extended periods of psycho-therapy, clients have the same problems, or that earlier problems may have been replaced by new ones. Moreover, when we look at the enormous consumption of drugs in our contemporary society, ranging from opiates, marijuana and amphetamines at the illegal end of the spectrum to Valium, Prozac and other anti-depressant medications at the legal end – not to mention our consumption of alcohol, tobacco and caffeine – we see that the majority of people are not capable of enjoying life without some kind of intoxicant or sedative.

It is my contention that if we want to experience a natural and lasting state of well-being, a different form of therapy is needed, a therapy that leads towards meditation. Why? Because even if we discover the historical origin of a problem, we still need to learn to become less identified with what is happening to us now, in the present moment. However, before moving in that direction, I would like to say a little more about mind itself.

The Roots of the Mind

If anthropologists are to be believed, the part of our mind that is uniquely human began its formation with our separation from the ape and gorilla families, about ten million years ago, and more recently with our evolution into modern form, as homo sapiens, about 120,000 years ago in Africa.

When we take into account that human beings are physically quite fragile and vulnerable creatures – compared to, say, a lion, an elephant, or a buffalo — it is not difficult to comprehend that in those ancient times the most valuable survival weapon in man's hands was his own mind. The thinking mechanism set him above other animals, allowing him to invent spears, bows and arrows, clubs and knives, together with a whole range of protective defenses such as walls, ditches, ramparts, moats and fire to keep wild beasts away while he rested and slept.

In other words, our modern mind has ancient roots that are primarily concerned with survival, self-protection and guarding against attack. These roots are basically fear-oriented. Even today, the ingrained habit of the mind is to continually make sure we are secure and safe, because deep down in its roots, it doubts that this is so. Deep down, it has not yet realized that modern technology has created human history's safest, coziest, best-fed form of society — at least, in Western countries.

Looking at this phenomenon through the terminology of trauma healing therapy, we might say that, collectively, we are all living in a state of permanent post-traumatic stress, because this is precisely what a trauma symptom is: one behaves in the present as if a past danger is still with us, and so we repeat a certain stress response endlessly without realizing that the danger is over.

Simply said, mind is a chronic worrier and when it has no problems to worry about it worries about *that*, and tends to imagine or create new problems:

You've got the rent covered this month...? Yes....But what about your credit card payments...? No problem, they're covered, too.... Okay, but the company's sales performance isn't looking good for the third quarter in succession... what if you are made redundant...? How's your pension plan...? And medical insurance cover...? And how about those headaches you're getting...? maybe it's a tumor... how's Mary going to manage with the kids when I'm gone...?

It is an old habit from the era of dark nights, wild beasts and tough times for homo sapiens. Seen from this perspective, it's not so surprising that, in the name of self-protection, we have created enough nuclear weapons to destroy the entire world seven times over. We need to feel absolutely sure that we have enough firepower in our arsenal to destroy the threat – from wherever it may come.

This is one aspect of mind to be considered. People with problems such as anxiety, stress and depression can take comfort from the fact that they are not solely responsible as individuals for their situation. Evolution of our species has given us an ingenious machine that can be extremely helpful, but it comes to us with a downside: a tendency towards worry, fear and paranoia. It's part of our evolutionary package and may explain why, in all our social history, we have never been so safe and secure as we are today, and yet have never been so stressed-out.

Living in Past and Future

The other aspect of mind that we need to examine is its tendency to live in either the past or the future. For example, you are walking along the beach on a sunny morning; you are relatively fit, with no serious medical problems; you have had your breakfast, you are well-clothed and warm. In this moment, just walking by the sea, there is no need for mind at all; there is no need for any thinking process. In this present moment, here and now, there are no problems and, in theory at least, you are free to simply relax and enjoy the walk.

Can you do it? Just try it and see. For a short time, as you step out of your car and onto the beach, you experience a few moments of being present, appreciating the fresh air, the sun shining on the waves, the free time at your disposal, but then, as you get into the rhythm of walking, thoughts start to arise in your mind. They come either in the form of memories from the past, or plans for the future:

You remember other walks... with other people... maybe with a girlfriend... years ago... this reminds you of how you broke up with her... you remember the argument... driving home in angry silence... meeting someone new... not so glamorous, but nice... she had a dog... and this reminds you... you have promised to buy a dog for your son for his birthday... in two weeks time... but which breed to choose... Golden Retriever, Labrador, German Shepherd... what about a kennel... buy one or build one...?

The association of thoughts, one giving rise to the next, absorbs you so that you entirely forget about the present moment. Your body is walking along the beach, your feet are hitting the sand, your lungs are inhaling the salty sea air, but your mind is far away... and you are identified with your mind, not with your body.

In a way, we can say that mind and reality never meet; they live in two different dimensions, because reality exists only in the present moment and mind exists in past and future.

So then, if my assessment of the nature of the human mind is accepted, it can be said that we are equipped with a thought-generating machine that is essentially neurotic, or fear-oriented, and which rarely, if ever, connects with reality. Moreover, we are so closely identified with the thoughts it generates that we never see ourselves as separate from them. One more thing to note: we can't turn it off. From the time we wake up in the morning until the time we sleep at night, the mind is in continuous action, a nonstop internal radio playing past memories and future dreams.

States of Well-Being

This is the downside, which I am emphasizing here because it is related to the issue of effective therapy, which is the subject of this book. The upside, as I have already indicated, is that we are blessed with a mind that can produce sophisticated linguistic communication, all kinds of inventions, technologies, poetry, art, architecture, music... and so on. I am not recommending that we dispense with the mind, even if it were possible to do so, but to recognize that it has certain limitations, and one of them is that mind is not good at relaxing into a state of well-being.

How, then, do we know that such states of well-being exist?

We know, because we've all been there. In spite of the mind's best efforts to keep us preoccupied with its own concerns, we have all had moments in life when we have been free of the grip of the mind, in a state of being. I call it 'being' rather than 'well-being' because the two terms are synonymous. When we are in a state of 'being' we naturally feel well-being.

Often, these moments come in a moment of surprise, or

wonder, or experiencing an unexpected turn of events. Consider this account of a traveling journalist, who was about to enter Israel:

For several days before my arrival, and also on the plane, I kept going over the moment when I would face Israeli immigration, because my passport was only two months from expiry and they usually insist on a minimum validity of six months. Moreover, I was coming from Dubai, which is politically opposed to Israel, and the stamp was clearly visible. And this was my third visit inside a year, so it looked suspicious... why so many visits if I'm not Jewish? I was sure they'd take me to a back room, put me through a long interrogation and maybe not let me stay.

There was a big crowd at immigration control at Tel Aviv airport. I must have waited in line for half-an-hour, still trying to figure out the best thing to say, rehearsing the lines, checking my story for loopholes, then suddenly it was my turn and I stepped up to the booth and handed over my passport. The young guy on duty looked at my name... "Richard Jeffries?" he asked. I nodded, "That's me." "Welcome to Israel." He stamped a page and waved me through. Within minutes I was in a taxi and heading downtown.

I couldn't believe it. I sat in the taxi dumb-struck, or 'gob-smacked' as kids say in the UK. All that worrying and mind-fucking... for nothing! A wave of relief washed over me and I settled into the back seat and just smiled. That was the most enjoyable taxi ride of my life.

This is just one example. Seeing a beautiful sunset, becoming utterly absorbed watching a child playing, getting an 'all-clear' from a doctor after a cancer scare... these are moments when we can enter a different dimension from the normal thinking process of the mind. Something takes our attention so completely that there is no space for the mind to come in. Or, something happens that is so unexpected, so surprising that the mind cannot grasp it;

we are jolted out of habitual thinking, into the moment, into reality.

A Fundamental Shift into the Present

This is the state of being I am talking about, and this is the state we want to emulate in the kind of therapy I am proposing. We are not simply trying to help a person find a certain harmony or resolution within the mind; rather, we aim at something more fundamental: to help him, or her, come out of identification with mind and its problem-creating nature.

In the state of being, real life situations do not change, but the 'problem' orientation of the client can shift significantly. For example, the pain of a broken relationship is still felt, but the client gains distance from the constant 'chewing' of the mind over past memories, feelings of regret, lost opportunities, hopes of reunion, fears of custody battles... all mixed up with the actual fact that a partner has gone.

In order to be in a state of being, one needs to say 'yes' to the present moment, because this is the only way to be in reality – reality, by definition, exists only in the present. Being, reality and 'yes' are three dimensions of one phenomenon. Moreover, saying 'yes' to the present is an acceptance of the situation, or issue, affecting the client, rather than denying, struggling, or fighting with it.

We will go into these issues in more depth in the following chapters. The important point to understand here is that 'mind' and 'being' are two separate states that never meet, and that healing happens more effectively and deeply in a state of being. Why? Because, as we have seen, mind is a state of unease, while being is a state of resting at home in oneself.

Exercise: 'Yes' to This Moment

This is a simple exercise that I do in my workshops to help people experience a state of being, rather than a state of mind. When we say 'yes' to this moment, the mind loses much of its need to function, because its habit is to want something else, desire a better future, or compare this moment with the past.

Before starting the exercise, make sure you are going to be undisturbed for the next 15-20 minutes, and can move around freely in a private space – either indoors or outdoors – and can also speak aloud without attracting attention from others. It is helpful to use a timer, or alarm, so that you do not need to continuously check the time.

When you are ready, begin to move, walking around, allowing your body to do whatever it likes. Now say aloud, "If I say 'yes' to myself in this moment, I am….." and then complete the sentence by describing whatever you find yourself doing in the present moment. For example, you may say, '"If I say 'yes' to myself in this moment, my arms are raised and stretching forward." Or, "If I say yes to myself in this moment, I am yawning."

Each sentence starts in the same way and is completed according to whatever you do. You may feel like shrugging your shoulders, laughing, frowning, dancing, rolling around on the floor… Each action should be spontaneous, without calculation or prior intention.

After 15 minutes, stop, close your eyes, and observe your inner state. Most people notice a change in attitude or mood, when they say 'yes' in this way. They become lighter and more carefree, because for a few minutes they have not been involved with concerns about past and future.

Chapter Three

Presence: A Healing Force

Presence is something we usually attribute to others, especially to actors, royalty and spiritual leaders, but rarely to ourselves. For example, after watching a great actor, like Sir Laurence Olivier, in a classic Shakespearian movie like "Richard III," we may comment, 'Sir Laurence had a commanding presence throughout the film'." Or, we may attend an audience with the Dalai Lama and note that his Tibetan Buddhist devotees were awed by his "divine presence."

In the context of healing, we may attribute this quality to a physician, therapist, shaman, or faith-healer, sensing a certain well-being in the presence of this person, even if we do not know, or even particularly like him. It is for this reason that Grigory Rasputin grew to have immense influence over Czar Nicholas II and his family, because through his healing presence Rasputin was able to stop the bleeding of the czar's son and heir, who was a hemophiliac.

More generally, we may notice that we feel good when a certain person is around, sensing that, as a result, our own inner state becomes more silent, more relaxed, more at peace. Something in us is touched through this person's presence and we feel an inner expansion, lightness, warmth, or sense of well-being that is beyond the usual feeling of liking someone, beyond the level of personality.

Presence and Being Present
Presence is not only a gift from birth, although some people do seem to be born with this quality. It can be acquired, it can be discovered within ourselves, because it manifests when we are

rooted in the 'here and now,' when we are not involved with dreams or thoughts about the past and future. Presence, in short, is a quality of being present, hence the similarity between the two terms.

The more a person is connected with the present moment, the more presence he will manifest. The more he is busy with thoughts, the less presence will radiate from him. This is something we all know from our day-to-day relating with friends, business colleagues and acquaintances. When we are talking with someone and he is only partly listening – his attention is wandering here and there, noticing a pretty woman passing by, continuously checking his mobile phone and so on – we do not feel his presence, we do not feel connected with him, or even respected. But when someone is really listening with his full attention we immediately feel better, because he is attentive not only to our words but to our being.

The quality of 'presence' is related to meditation, as was noted in chapter one, which can be defined as the art of watching the mind and dissociating from the thinking process. A meditator is, by definition, someone who is oriented towards the 'here and now' and not caught up in past memories or future dreams. He can be present, and so he has presence.

Operating from Presence

However, we need to make a distinction between a person's general ability to be present, which is related to his experience of meditation, and whether he is in touch with this quality at a certain moment or not. This means that a person may have the ability to be present, but is vulnerable to being distracted by thoughts or worries. Later in the book, we will see the importance of making this distinction when working with people.

Most good therapists operate from a space of presence and make sure they are in this state when working with a client. They create a distance to their own mental preoccupations during a session, rooting themselves in the present moment. From this state, they are able to notice whether — and in what moments — the client is also present. A session in which a client remains continuously in the mind is likely to be more tiring and difficult; for example, when the client talks at length about his, or her, 'problems' in a descriptive or narrative way, telling stories about past events, without contacting his real feelings. As we shall see, it is the job of a good therapist to bring a client to the present and avoid story-telling.

Connecting to a Meditative Space

The importance of presence in therapy has been noted by Sagarpriya Delong, who has given this phenomenon a different name; she has called it 'resonance,' indicating a person's connection to a meditative space that is beyond the personal. For example, if two people are both present, or 'in resonance,' they will not feel any sense of separation, because they are both tuned to the same transpersonal space; rather, they will experience an inner expansion and a state of oneness with the other.

In Sagarpriya's approach, the therapist begins by reading the client's general state of resonance, which refers to the client's ability to be present and in contact with his own being. This information allows the therapist to be realistic about what is possible in the course of a session with a client, in terms of depth and the issues that can be addressed. So 'resonance' creates a foundation for the session and gives a direction to follow.

We need to note the distinction between Sagarpriya's use of the term 'resonance' and its more common meaning. Generally speaking, resonance refers to our capacity to sense what someone else is sensing, to tune into another person and understand what he, or she, is feeling. A therapist may do this with a client, for example, suddenly experiencing a sense of loss, or grief, or perhaps an unfamiliar pain in the heart, or stomach, then discovering that these sensations are mirroring what is happening in the client.

Sagarpriya's use of the term is more restricted and, as indicated, refers to the client's ability to be in a state of presence, with or without the company of others, resonating with a transpersonal state. While acknowledging her creation of a specific term to indicate the importance of presence in therapy, it will avoid confusion and be more convenient in this book if we continue to use the word 'presence.'

The Foundation of a Session

As a prior condition to helping a client find presence, a therapist needs to know how to find this quality in himself. This is the foundation on which to build a session, otherwise the therapist will be distracted by the chatter and commentaries of his own mind, rather like a leaf blown in the wind, without clear direction. As presence is related to meditation, an authentic therapist will need to have experience in meditation before being able to help a client find presence.

It also needs to be understood that presence is not related to any particular activity. One can be present while working, dancing, eating, sitting silently... and one can also be *not* present in these same activities. It is not the act itself that is important, but the state of consciousness of the individual.

The main difficulty in an inter-active situation, such as a counseling session, is that a therapist's attention naturally goes towards the other person — after all, he wants to 'help' the client — and in doing so he forgets himself. Presence, however, is a consequence of remembering oneself. So, rather than being focused solely on the client, a therapist also needs to remain connected with himself.

Finding Presence: Five Hints

Before beginning a session with a client, or during the session itself, the therapist can follow these five hints for finding presence. They can be done in sequence, or can be used separately, since each one is capable of inviting a state of presence independently of the others. They are useful not only for those working with people, but also in general for anyone who is attracted to the challenge of being more present in his, or her, life.

The five hints:

1. Find your body position
2. Become aware of your breathing.
3. Relax into your heart.
4. Remember a moment of meditation.
5. Follow an impulse that arises after observing the other steps.

1. Body Position

The body is always in the present, in the 'here and now.' It is through the body that we experience being alive; it is through our physical senses that we experience reality as it is, moment to moment. The body can, therefore, be of great help in finding and maintaining a state of presence - because it is already in this condition. At any moment, we can pause, stop what we are doing, take a moment to become aware of body sensations and in this way enter the present moment.

Apart from cosmetic concerns about "how do I look?" we tend to forget about our bodies, taking them for granted until something goes wrong. For example, we don't usually think about our backs until one day the lumbar muscles suddenly go into acute spasm and leave us lying helplessly on our backs, waiting for the doctor.

As soon as we pay attention to feeling the body, becoming aware of our physical nature, we come into the present, and we also remember that we have an inner sense that tells us if the body is well and in a suitable position. During a session, it is helpful for a therapist to remain aware of his, or her body position, checking in, once in a while, to note whether the body is feeling comfortable. Trying to be 'comfortable' does not mean that one lies down while the client is talking, but it can mean that the therapist may take a moment to stand up, or stretch. In other words, we dispose of the conventional idea of how a professional therapist should behave - sitting 'correctly' throughout a session without moving — but instead trusting one's own inner sense of what the body needs and using this as a vehicle to remain present.

2. Awareness of Breathing

After checking one's body position, place attention on the breathing. Traditional Buddhist schools have used this method for centuries to train people in the art of meditation.

The Buddhist Vipassana meditation is focused on watching one's own breath, noticing air flowing into the body and then out again. Some Buddhist schools focus attention on the rise and fall of the belly with the in-breath and out-breath, while others focus on the nostrils, noticing cool air entering through the nose on the in-breath and warm air exiting on the out-breath.

The breath is something that connects us to the moment—one cannot breathe in the past or future; it is always a here-and-now process.

It is also interesting to note that people who are deeply involved in a thought process tend to breathe in a shallow way, seemingly hardly breathing at all. On the other hand, people who are in a hurry, or who appear anxious, often breath at a faster rate than seems natural.

Each of us has a breathing rhythm that is natural and relaxed, and this is also reflected in the rhythm at which we speak and the pace at which we move. When we focus attention on our natural rhythm of breathing we can also tell if the body wants to be still, or perhaps move in some subtle way, and this will also help us to come out of the mind and into presence.

In other words, when a therapist is with a client, it is helpful for him to follow his own rhythm, without feeling obliged to sit quietly or to follow the rhythm of the client.

3. Relaxing into the Heart

After spending a few moments, or minutes, focusing awareness on the breathing, one can shift attention to the heart center, in the middle of the chest. This is not the physical location of the biological heart, but the energy center of the spiritual heart.

When we feel connected to the heart, thinking tends to slow down and even stop for a few moments. As a result, we are more in touch with what is happening here and now. An effective way to remember the heart is to imagine that one is letting go of the head and mind, focusing instead on the heart center and inviting it to relax.

In this space, it is also possible to imagine that one is "listening from the heart" while the client is talking. It can be an interesting experience to compare this form of listening with the usual way of hearing, in which we are trying to understand the other with the mind, from a conceptual or rational point of view. One can imagine as if the ears are directly connected to the heart.

This exercise can be tried at any moment in daily life and it is significant to observe the effect it has on the person to whom we are listening. Often, the person feels more received and understood. This is because the heart is the center of transformation and is capable of turning negative feelings and beliefs into positive ones. This is where the real alchemy of transformation can happen.

4. Remember a Moment of Meditation

The therapist closes his eyes and recalls a moment, a situation, when he had an experience of deep meditation in the past. To remember this 'peak experience' of meditation and perhaps to also visualize it, including all the sensations, sounds and maybe smells, is an effective way to rekindle those qualities in the present moment. It may have been a moment of aloneness in nature, or sitting in front of a spiritual master, or when relaxing after strenuous activity. One can use the remembrance of that moment to penetrate the present moment.

5. Follow an Impulse

After one has observed these hints, finding the right body position, becoming aware of the breathing and relaxing the heart, it will be easier to experience moments of spontaneous action that are not coming from preconceived ideas or rational inferences. Such impulses arise as a response to the present moment, from one's inner being, and we can intuitively feel these impulses. When we act from presence we do things at the right time, in the right moment, not too early and not too late.

There are therapists who are in too much of a hurry to achieve a result with a client, and so they do not allow enough gaps in which spontaneous impulses can arise; there are also therapists who are afraid to act outside a set format of procedure and so they let the impulse pass, holding back their spontaneity.

To be connected to the present does not mean to only sit silently. It means to act when the moment requires, to wait for the right time and then follow an impulse when it arises.

Guided Meditations that Support Presence

Here are a series of exercises that are related to the above hints, which support the experience of presence. Each exercise lasts for 15-20 minutes, unless otherwise stated.

Guided Meditation 1: Saying 'Yes' to the Body

This is a variation to the technique given at the end of the previous chapter.

Begin by discovering what your body wants to do right now. Take a position, standing, sitting or lying down, and check if it feels right. If it doesn't feel right, change it. Now check to see if your place in the room feels right, or if you need to be somewhere else. Experiment. Go to different places in the room and notice where you feel more relaxed, more at ease, more happy.

While doing this, notice moments when you may feel a little lost. These moments are important. If there is no clear sequence of instructions, or directions, the first thing that happens is that we tend to feel lost. That's okay. Look inside and ask yourself "What is good for me?" "What is good for my body?"

Feel whether your body wants to move, or be still, and if you are not sure, experiment. Be like a curious child, ready to explore. You can also make sounds. You can move a little faster, then a little slower, until you find the rhythm you enjoy most.

After 15-20 minutes, check your level of satisfaction. If it is below 60-70 percent then explore for another 10 minutes to see how you can make this moment more enjoyable.

Follow the body.

You can do this exercise alone, or with others.

Guided Meditation 2: Internal Observation

Find a position where your body feels good, preferably sitting or standing; if you lie down, you may feel drowsy and go to sleep. Create a space in your schedule when you will not be disturbed.

Observe what is going on in your body, any sensations that you may notice, such as a slight tingling or streaming sensation in the fingers, arms, legs, or at the back of your neck, or any tension in the shoulders, or in your back, or feelings of 'warm' or 'cold' in different areas of your body...

Allow these sensations to be as they are, without trying to change them in any way.

Notice the place where your feet are in contact with the ground, or where your buttocks are resting on a cushion, or where your hands and arms may be touching the rest of your body... notice any sensations in these areas, without trying to change anything. Notice the area of your chest and heart, paying attention to the rhythm of your breathing, the movement of your rib cage and the beating of your heart.

Notice the places where your body feels discomfort and where it feels at ease and well.

Become aware of your body as a whole and feel if there is any slight impulse or small movement that your body wants to do. Let it happen without any effort on your part.

Now become aware of the space inside you from where you can be a witness to all of this. Sensations are happening in your body, changes are going on continuously, but the space from which you witness all of this remains the same; it is unchanging and unaffected by anything.

Now see if you can be aware of both simultaneously: the sensations in your body and the witnessing consciousness that is beyond them.

Guided Meditation 3: Rocking the Pelvis
Stand in a comfortable, relaxed position, wearing loose clothing. Your feet should be shoulder-width apart and firmly planted on the ground, so that your body can move without disturbing your balance. Bare feet on a wooden floor is best.

Inhale deeply through your mouth, feeling the breath entering your throat, passing down into your chest and imagining that it continues all the way down into your belly. Imagine as if your in-breath is filling your belly.

When you feel your in-breath reaching your belly, notice how the belly needs more space and your pelvis naturally begins to tilt backwards.

As you breathe out, the pelvis will swing forwards, back to it original position and maybe a little further.

Allow your pelvis to rock in accordance with your breath, swinging back with the in-breath and forward with the out-breath. You can picture yourself in a rocking chair: your pelvis is like the chair, swinging back and forward.

Give yourself time to connect with this sensation, closing your eyes and feeling this rocking movement that follows your breathing. It is important to keep your knees unlocked and slightly bent, otherwise your pelvis cannot move easily. Also, make sure that your feet are in line with your shoulders, not too far apart and not too close together. After a few minutes, allow your arms to follow this movement, swinging back and forward with the pelvis and the breath. The main movement comes from the pelvis; the rest of the body follows. There is no real effort. The in-breath is moving your body and you allow and slightly encourage it.

Continue rocking for 10-15 minutes. Then, take 5 minutes to rest, either standing or lying on your back, and observe what has happened in your body and how you feel.

Guided Meditation 4: Heart Meditation

Stand or sit comfortably in a relaxed way, with your eyes closed.

Focus your attention on the center of your chest, your spiritual heart.

Imagine a small ball is located in the center of your chest and give it a color.

With each breathe inhaled, imagine the ball is slowly growing bigger, like a balloon being filled with air. Let this ball grow slowly out of your chest, in time with the rhythm of your breathing.

Slowly, let it expand beyond the boundaries of your body.

Use your hands, as if you can touch the balloon as it begins to grow beyond your chest and body.

Imagine your whole body becomes engulfed inside the ball and your hands are eventually touching it from the inside. Let it grow bigger than the room, bigger than the area in which you live, bigger than the whole world.

Feel that everyone and everything is included in your heart.

Then, slowly allow the ball to shrink until it is again inside your chest. Again, following the rhythm of your breathing, imagine the out-breath is slowly taking the air out of the balloon. Become aware of the source and center of the ball. Even while it is growing or shrinking, this center remains unmoving.

Feel this center for a moment, then slowly open your eyes.

Guided Meditation 5: Spontaneity with a Partner

This is a partner exercise that encourages spontaneity in the presence of another person.

Stand opposite your partner with eyes open, looking at each other in a soft, receptive way. Let your body be loose and relaxed. Be aware that your breathing is easy and natural.

Notice any impulse that comes to you while standing in front of your partner. Follow the impulse without knowing why, or thinking about where it will lead, without holding back or exaggerating the movement. This can include any gestures and also touch, but should not involve any other objects.

This is not a 'mirror' exercise. You are not copying each other. You have no intention to act in a specific way, either towards your partner, or towards yourself. There is no need to be 'funny' or entertain your partner; in fact, you are not concerned about the other, or about what he, or she, is thinking. You are simply 'listening' for impulses that arise inside you and following them.

If there is no impulse, stand and wait in a relaxed way. Trust your body and your spontaneity. You can include sounds, but do not use any words or try to communicate.

Notice when an impulse wants to end and do not try to prolong it. Allow gaps, where nothing is happening. Go with what happens by itself, without letting the mind interfere, and remain watchful.

After 5-10 minutes come back to yourself, closing your eyes and turning away from your partner, so you are alone. Continue to follow any impulses for another 5 minutes. Notice if there is any difference when you do it alone.

Finding Presence: Valuable in Itself

Finding presence is essential if one wants to work with people. Guided meditations help a therapist to find presence, but during a session it is neither necessary nor practical to follow a whole exercise. A simple remembrance, or a moment of tuning into one's own body, breathing, or heart, is usually enough to become alert, present and centered.

When a therapist is present it helps the client to also come to this moment. One can encourage this by asking the client how he feels in his body, tracking his body sensations, or reminding him to notice his breathing, or asking what he feels in the moment, rather than getting lost in story-telling or analysis.

It is also helpful to reflect back to a client what one sees in him, or her, simply mirroring the other. All this can be done without any specific therapeutic technique or methodology. Without helping someone to solve a difficulty, one can help a person to come out of the normal, routine functioning of the mind into presence, which in itself is valuable.

Finding presence is important not only in counseling, but in every life situation. It is a way to shift one's state of consciousness from thinking to being.

Chapter Four

The Nature of Desire

Legend has it that towards the end of the 12th century A.D. a young man growing up close to the Onon River in Mongolia had a dream. He dreamed that it was his destiny to unite all the warring nomadic tribes in the Mongolian region of Asia and lead them in a conquest of the entire world. His name was Temujin, later to become known as Genghis Kahn. By the time he died in 1227, he was the ruler of the largest contiguous empire that human history had ever seen.

His descendants went still further, stretching the Mongol Empire across Europe, Asia and the Middle East. None of them succeeded in conquering the world, but that did not stop them from trying. Nor has it discouraged others from acting out similar ambitions: Alexander, Julius Caesar, Tamerlane, Napoleon, Joseph Stalin, Adolf Hitler...

It is easy, in retrospect, to categorize such people as a special group of 'madmen' or 'tyrants' who somehow get into power and create disasters for others. But that is not how these phenomena happen. People like Genghis Kahn are not alone in their dreams and desires. Their dynastic ambitions somehow find resonance in the minds of thousands, or millions of people, who willingly follow them.

The truth is, we all have within us the same mechanism of desire, and whether it is an ambition to be a world conqueror, or just to have a more fashionable pair of sunglasses than your friend sitting across the table at your local café, makes no real difference. It is only a question of degree. The mechanism is the same.

The Nature of Mind is 'Wanting'

In order to understand the functioning of the human mind, we need to understand and study the mechanism of 'desire.' Basically, the nature of mind is 'wanting,' wanting more of something, wanting something other than what we have. The object of wanting doesn't really matter; it may be a material object, a powerful position in life, a woman or a man, or it may be a spiritual ambition, such as wanting to be an enlightened being, a wise sage before whom others will bow down and pay homage.

The moment anything becomes of interest to the mind it becomes a desire, and this 'interest' or 'wanting' has no limits, no end. There is an ancient parable, which Osho loved to tell in his discourses, that illustrates the essential nature of the problem:

A great king had a habit of rising early each morning and going for a walk in his beautiful garden, just outside the palace, where he could be alone and at peace with himself. One morning however, as he walked into the garden, he saw a beggar standing there, waiting for him.

"What do you want?" asked the king, annoyed at this intrusion.

In answer, the beggar held out his begging bowl and said, "I have a simple request: that you fill this bowl with anything. It does not matter with what... rocks, dirt, sand... anything you like."

The king felt insulted and replied, "Do you think I am so poor a king that I cannot fill your little bowl with anything more than dirt? I will fill it with gold and then you will see with whom you are dealing."

The beggar held up a cautionary hand and said, "Think twice, great king, it is not too late to change your mind. You do not have to agree to my request."

But the king would not listen. He clapped his hands, summoned his servants and told them to fill the beggar's bowl with gold coins. Immediately, they brought from the king's treasury a bag of gold coins and poured them into the bowl, whereupon they instantly disappeared, leaving the bowl empty.

The king was astonished, but refused to be defeated. He told his servants to bring all the bags of gold in his treasury and pour them into the bowl, which was done, but as the contents of each bag poured into the bowl, the coins disappeared.

Still, the king refused to acknowledge his defeat. He ordered his servants to bring diamonds, rubies, pearls... all the jewels in his treasury and pour them into the bowl. Again, as the sacks of jewels were emptied into the bowl, the precious stones all disappeared.

The king was ruined, all his treasure was exhausted, and still the bowl was empty. Humbled, he fell down at the feet of the beggar and asked forgiveness, saying "Tell me, what is the secret of this bowl, that it can receive all the riches of the world and yet cannot be filled?"

The beggar laughed and replied, "It is no secret. This bowl is made from the skull of a human being. It is made from the desiring mind. That is why it can never be satisfied, never be filled."

One can see the damaging effects of this phenomenon not only in our personal relationships, but on a vast scale around the earth. Even today, the insanity of wanting more is eating up the resources of this planet, destroying its natural beauty, polluting its atmosphere and water to the extent that we are endangering our own survival.

It is easy to point the finger at people like Hitler and Napoleon, condemning them as 'megalomaniacs,' but the truth is that our modern consumer society, based on an economic system that sustains itself by constantly fueling our desire for more, is inflicting more damage on this planet than any aspiring world conqueror, and we are all participants in it.

Desire is Related to 'No'

Let us examine the psychology behind desire. Desire is always related to a 'no' to this moment. In fact, this is the reason we desire something, because that which is happening already, right now, in this very moment, is not experienced as sufficient or fulfilling. We do not want *this*, we want *that*... something else, something more.

Why do we want something else? Why do we so easily dismiss that which is available now, in favor of that which we desire? The basic reason is that we do not know ourselves, we do not possess ourselves; the path to our innermost consciousness, to our being, is blocked and that is why we look outwards for fulfillment, as a kind of substitute. There is a black hole inside us that we try to fill but somehow never succeed.

Individual seekers down the ages have attained to self-knowing and self-fulfillment – Gautam Buddha, Jalaluddin Rumi, Saint Francis of Assisi, Ramana Maharshi and many others – but no organized religion has been able to guide people towards this experience. On the contrary, religious leaders down the ages have joined hands with political rulers to prevent self-inquiry, because it suits the vested interests of every society to keep the masses ignorant of themselves and therefore weak, enslaved, dependent and obedient.

This is not the place to go into all the aspects of this issue, but we can say that, as individuals, our loss of being and orientation towards outer fulfillment begins as children, with our conditioning.

Learning Not to Value Ourselves

Conditioning means 'learning.' To use the analogy of a computer, it refers to the programming of the bio-computer inside our heads. It is social programming in the name of 'education' and represents the totality of all we are told as growing children by our parents, teachers, priests, opinion-makers, moralists... in short, by society. This is how social values are passed from generation to generation; our parents were handed down similar values from their parents and so on. With the best of intentions, our parents turn us away from ourselves and towards the glittering prizes offered to us in the form of social acceptance, public recognition, successful careers, wealth, prestige, power… and so on.

We learn not to value ourselves as individuals, but to measure ourselves against external standards that are established through comparison and competition with others: who comes first in the class, who gets highest points in the exam, which team wins the game, who gets the most attractive-looking girlfriend, who goes to the best university, who obtains the highest-paying job.

An essential part of this process is the acquired understanding that we are not good enough as we are. We need to be better, stronger, faster, more sexual, more attractive, more intelligent, more wealthy… We absorb these ideas so deeply that we cannot distinguish anymore what really comes from within, as an authentic reflection of our individuality, and what has been given to us.

Society has given beautiful names to this chronically stressful condition, like 'idealism,' which suggests that we should always be looking beyond where we are towards the horizon, creating a bigger, better, brighter future for ourselves. In the USA it is characterized as the 'American Dream,' an invitation to create lofty personal goals and then try our utmost to get there, whatever the cost; and remember the saying, "If at first you don't succeed, try, try, try again." So the energy behind desire is effort, the effort to get what one desires, in the belief that this will bring the fulfillment that society has promised.

On a certain level, in terms of motivating us to expand and explore our personal potential, this strategy can be effective. But in terms of creating an authentic sense of personal fulfillment and a relaxed state of well-being, it doesn't work. Behind every ideal, every longing, every desire, there is tension and anxiety, because we are rejecting ourselves as we are now, rejecting what is available to us now, in favor of ambitious goals that we may never reach.

In terms of the physical body, desire usually manifests as physical tension, because the body follows the ambitions of the mind and tries to suck or pull the desired object closer to itself. In order to do this, it has to physically contract. So an experienced therapist can see the language of desire written in the posture and alignment of the client's body.

Happy Dreams, Broken Dreams

A state of desire is a state of visualizing the future. People who are caught up in the energy of desire may appear determined and strong, or dreamy and idealistic, or miserable and sad, but in any case they are not connected to reality.

In a session, clients in this state can be recognized in two ways. First, they may have wide open eyes and appear happy and excited because they are visualizing what they want to attain or acquire in the future. Second, people may appear miserable and sad, because they are aware that right now they do not have what they desire.

So desire is accompanied either by misery or by a kind of happiness related to dreaming. Often, such people alternate between these two states, hoping optimistically and appearing happy, then sinking into frustration and misery. This cycle continues until the individual becomes interested in exploring the present moment.

But why do we all continue to desire so much, if in reality it is an unpleasant experience? First, we need to understand that in order to comprehend the effort and the tension behind desire, we need to look 'in,' inside ourselves, instead of looking 'out' at the world around us and at the objects of desire. Usually, however, we are so focused on externals that we forget to look in, and this is understandable because our modern society is continuously feeding us with new desires: consumer products, bargains, sales, job opportunities, dating services, self-improvement courses…

Many times, we are able to get what we want. We get the job

we want, the house or love partner we dreamed about, and then we experience a short period of satisfaction and fulfillment. We may become aware of the underlying tension only when the euphoria has passed, the honeymoon ends, the bills pile up, or when we develop some kind of stress-related mental or physical illness. Then we may recognize that essentially we are as unfulfilled as before.

Fear of Loss

When a person stops looking outward and becomes curious to investigate his own inner world, one of the first feelings that arises is a fear of loss, of losing whatever status and possessions have been acquired through struggle and effort. The focus is shifting and the future seems more uncertain, one's old assumptions are being questioned and the totality of one's personal drive towards ambition and achievement slackens off. You are entering unfamiliar territory and the direction life may take is unknown; it is no more a laid out plan where everything is decided and fixed. The partner may leave, someone else may get the promotion, income may be less when one takes time for meditation, or one may not be so respected when one does not do what everyone else is doing.

This is the risk and it may bring up fear, because life now feels more insecure – rather, life is now recognized in its true colors as an essentially insecure, moment-to-moment phenomenon — and this can be frightening. So it is tempting to close the door to one's inner world and go back to the former lifestyle that gives the illusion of safety and security. This is one of the reasons why people turn away from meditation, especially if they have become strongly attached to all that they have acquired.

Suppressing Unwelcome Feelings

When a person looks into his inner world and explores what lies behind his desires, he may become aware of the effort he has been making to reach somewhere, or to hold on to something. If he has the courage to pass through the fear of losing all this, allowing himself to relax more deeply and continuing to look inside, he will eventually discover that at the source of desire there is the phenomenon of rejection.

The reason for this rejection lies in the ideals that he has been given through his social conditioning. For example, if a man thinks of himself as a kind person, he will want to reject any angry feelings if they begin to surface inside him; not only that, he will make great efforts to cultivate a 'kind' personality, which is nothing but a false mask, a pretension that hides a different reality underneath.

To give another example: if an individual cannot stand the feeling of loneliness, he will reject it by making great efforts to find a love partner and have a 'steady relationship,' and is likely to try and stay in a relationship at any cost, even if the togetherness is not rooted in love and creates nothing but misery.

Any experience, if it is not in accordance with what is socially acceptable, will tend to be rejected and the individual will want to fill that 'hole' with something from the outside, with a value that has been given to him by society. This is how desires are created.

In a society that values 'happy' people, any negative feelings will have to be rejected. Then people may appear to be 'happy,' but their happiness is false. In a society where to be a hard worker and attain a respectable position in life is valued, it will be difficult to enjoy oneself doing nothing, or feeling at ease in an ordinary job. If wealth is valued, great efforts will be made to obtain money and avoid any appearance of poverty. Whatever aspect of one's nature or inner reality is in conflict with social values, that part will tend to be disowned and replaced with a desire for something else.

At this point, something strange happens. People are given the ideal to be honest, to be truthful, to search for meaning in life, but it is precisely through these ideals that they become dishonest.

The more the individual tries to follow social convention, the more he is distracted from himself and so the more he will remain unfulfilled. Faced with the meaninglessness of whatever he has already attained, he will seek new goals in order to fill the inner emptiness, moving further and further away from himself.

But the parts of ourselves that we are rejecting never go away. All that happens is that these unwelcome experiences — loneliness, emptiness, meaninglessness, any disowned parts — are suppressed. They go 'underground,' disappearing out of conscious view into the subconscious and unconscious areas of our minds. Desire is a kind of running away, because we don't want to have certain experiences, and the reason why we don't want to have those experiences is because our conditioning tells us that it is not good to feel this way.

So beliefs and ideals lead to the rejection of actual experience. The problem is, however, that rejection can never lead to personal transformation. Essentially, it is a state of denial. How can we become healed and whole as individuals through pushing away those parts of ourselves that seem unattractive? Rather, we become split, schizophrenic, dividing our psyche into two parts that are in a continuous struggle with each other.

Transformation through Acceptance

Transformation happens through acceptance. We become whole when we accept an experience as it is, without trying to change it, or fix it, and this is possible only when we let go of any ideals and beliefs about how life should be… how *we* should be.

For example, when we accept our moments of loneliness, or anger, and start relaxing with them, saying 'yes' to what is, we give ourselves permission to discover for the first time what this state actually feels like. Loneliness may give us a sense of depth, anger may give us a sense of power and vitality… any experience has something to teach us, if we are willing to wholeheartedly embrace it. When we accept each experience as it manifests, or emerges from within, no desire is born out of it, because no desire arises out of saying 'yes' to what is.

Ordinarily, a person with clear goals and ambitions may appear positive, but seen from this perspective such a person is negative; he is saying 'no' to what is. The content of what he rejects is not so important — whether fear, anger, or sadness. The fact of saying 'no' is what matters.

When we work with a client in therapy, we want to help a person shift from saying 'no' to saying 'yes.' If, for example, a client comes with a problem of anger – "I want to drop my anger" — the main work will not be to help this client get rid of his anger, but, on the contrary, to say 'yes' to it, to understand it. Understanding something deeply is itself a transformative force, but this is not an effort, or a goal. The first step is to come to an agreement with how things are, rather than trying to change anything through effort or will power.

Gradually, over time, this brings real change and contains the whole science of inner transformation. A person who rejects anger will always remain angry. Maybe the anger will be deeply suppressed, behind a mask of rigid self-control, but it will persist, and it will find ways to leak out. Whatever we are against will remain.

The alchemy of inner transformation is to switch from 'no' to 'yes.' We also call it acceptance. A well-known book by the American poet, Walt Whitman, has the significant title "I Celebrate Myself." Whatever Whitman finds within himself he accepts and celebrates. If he is sad, he celebrates sadness; if angry, he celebrates that… and so on. This is an intelligent approach, because emotion is basically energy, and when we say 'yes' to energy, as it is, it has freedom to move, change and transform.

Examples from Sessions

A desire often hides the opposite reality. Here are two shortened pieces from typical session situations, where the initial desire is transformed through the acceptance of an experiential reality.

Example 1

Client: I want to be more open and loving towards people.

Therapist: What do you notice in yourself when you say that?

Client: I feel a lot of tension in my belly.

Therapist: Can you explore that a little more?

Client: There is an irritation, maybe even anger… I don't know where it comes from, but I don't like it.

Therapist: If you would allow that energy to spread out rather than pushing it down, what happens?

Client (sitting up straight and moving his body): There is a lot of energy in my body, I get hot. It actually doesn't feel so bad.

Therapist: Could you imagine sharing this energy with people?

Client (laughing): It is new, but I like the idea.

This is a typical example. The client has certain ideas about what openness and lovingness mean, and so he creates a rejection or repression of an inner experience. The more he tries to be 'open' the more tension is created; when he accepts and allows what he considers as 'unloving,' the desire to be different disappears and an authentic openness results.

Example 2:

Client: I really long to find a partner and be in a loving relationship.

Therapist: How do you feel right now?

Client: I feel a bit frustrated and sad, because whatever I do it doesn't seem to work and I have not met a suitable person for so long.

Therapist: How is it for you to be alone?

Client: I feel lonely.

Therapist: Would you like to find out more about this feeling, for a moment?

Client: When I go into this feeling, it is like entering into an abyss, it frightens me.

Therapist: Let's take a moment to stay with that, without entering this feeling too deeply. Observe all the sensations that you are aware of right now that go along with the feeling.

Client: My knees are shaky and I feel not so stable and grounded. I feel not so sure of myself.

Therapist: Yes, and how is that for you?

Client: Usually I avoid such feelings and make sure that I have things under control. But right now... it feels a little bit exciting not to know what comes next. I can feel a lot of energy passing through my legs now.

Therapist: Give yourself time to feel that.

(and later) It seems to me that not having a partner right now gives you a chance to feel and explore yourself more.

Client: I never saw it this way.

The client was making great efforts to get what he desired and, as he didn't succeed, frustration set in. The therapist does not explore the sadness that results from an unfulfilled desire, but looks for the rejected experiential reality underneath the desire. By owning it, together with related feelings of fear and uncertainty, the client gains inner strength and the experience of 'not being in a relationship' appears in a new light. It also shows here that strength is the result of accepting and owning fear, not of trying to avoid it.

In both these examples the client has come to the session with a certain desire. The work of the therapist is not to help the client fulfill his desire – to become more open, or to find a love partner – but to help him discover and explore the rejected energy and learn to accept and even welcome it. The therapist does not join the client in the dimension of desire, but, on the contrary, remains in a state of presence and invites the client to enter the same dimension. Eventually, this will lead to the dropping of the desire, or to the realization of desire on a higher plain – the realization that "this is what I really want." Real transformation is the result of understanding, not effort.

Exercise: Recognizing Desire

In a session, we need to distinguish between two states of happiness: one that is coming from a state of acceptance and one that is the result of the mind having achieved something it has desired. The latter is, of course, short-lived, as the desiring mind will again move toward the future, toward a new target or objective.

Here is a simple exercise that allows people to recognize the state of desire. It is done in pairs.

Partner A is asked to talk about the things that he, or she, desires. Each sentence begins with the phrase "I want..." and is completed with a description of the desired object.

Partner B listens silently, carefully watching the facial expressions and general mood of Partner A. Partner B also pays attention to any changes in his own inner state.

Partner A talks for 5-10 minutes.

When asked for feedback at the end of the exercise, Partner B, the one who has been watching, usually reports one of the following alternatives:

1. Partner A became excited and animated; his eyes became bigger, his smile wider, his gestures more pronounced. This is the state of happiness related to desire, generated by hope for the future.
2. Partner A became sad and miserable. This, again, is related to desire, but in this case the person became depressed because he felt the absence of the desired object, believing that this will never be achieved.

In both cases, Partner B often reports that, checking his own response to listening, nothing touched or moved him. Why? Because it can be boring or tiring, or both, to listen to another's desires. When this happens to a therapist in a session, it indicates that the client who is speaking is not in a state of saying 'yes' to the present moment, and this is valuable training for a therapist who will meet many clients in similar states of desire.

Either they will be hoping to get rid of a problem, or they will be depressed by the belief that this is not possible. When, however, a client's happiness is related to an acceptance of what is, a therapist will feel an inner expansion, his relaxation will deepen and there will be a feeling of connectedness with the client.

For a therapist, it is important to remain choice-less, noticing the different spaces, or states, that his clients bring to a session. Then he can be clear about what deserves his support and attention, and what simple needs to be ignored and not given energy.

When a client is in a state of desire, it means that energetically the therapist is alone. There will be no 'meeting' on the level of being while the client is in this state, because only one of the two is present.

It is part of a therapist's job to tolerate this situation, to drop any desire for a deeper connection with this client, otherwise the therapist, too, will move into a state of goal-orientation and future. He can invite the client to be present, through being present himself, which gives the client the opportunity to come out of the mind and into the moment without feeling pushed or manipulated.

Chapter Five

The Influence of Love

When we look at what really works and is of help to people in therapy and counseling, we need to recognize that love is one of the most important contributing factors. It has been said many times that love is the source of all healing, which sounds rather poetic and abstract in the hard-nosed, scientific age in which we live, but even science is beginning to acknowledge and support this conclusion.

Dr. Dean Ornish, an American cardiologist who became internationally known for his approach to reversing heart disease through the use of low fat, high carbohydrate diets, also observed that love, hugs and human warmth had a significant impact on unclogging arteries. At first, Ornish regarded this as a side issue, but later he helped conduct a study at Yale University involving 119 men and 40 women undergoing coronary angiography – an X-ray examination of the chambers of the heart. Those who felt the most loved and supported by their partners, families and friends had substantially less blockages in their heart arteries than the other subjects.

In a related study, researchers looked at almost 10,000 married men with no prior history of angina. These men had high levels of risk factors, such as elevated cholesterol, high blood pressure, diabetes, and electrocardiogram abnormalities. Those who felt their wives did not show them love experienced almost twice as much angina as the first group, who felt their wives did show them love.

So, in looking at love in the context of therapy, we are not orbiting away from practical matters into poetic fantasy. We are looking at a powerful human quality that is of tremendous significance in terms of health and healing.

The Many Dimensions of Love

There is also a biochemical aspect to love that has received increasing scrutiny in recent years. In 2004, for example, Helen Fisher, an anthropologist and research professor at Rutgers University, USA, identified three distinct dimensions of love, each with its own neurochemicals:

1. Lust, the craving for sexual gratification, is associated with testosterone in both sexes.
2. Intense romantic love that idealizes a particular partner is tied to dopamine, which has been linked to all kinds of addictions, including cocaine, heroin, alcohol and tobacco.
3. A calm, long-term and secure attachment to a partner is related to the hormones oxytocin and vasopressin.

Fisher asserted that each type of love is governed by a different brain system and they can all act independently. No wonder there is so much confusion about love and what it really means to us. In fact, sometimes we are not even clear if we love or hate the same person, feelings can change so fast.

We say we love our partner, our children, our parents and friends, but we also extend the phenomenon of love beyond human relationships, saying that we love our dog, car, breakfast cereal, coffee, job, country, or that we love to play tennis or go to the gym. Obviously, a single word cannot have the same meaning in all these different contexts. So when we talk about love in a therapeutic context, we need to have some understanding about the difference between conditioned love – meaning, love that is determined by our biology, survival instincts and social programming—-and an unconditional or unmotivated form of love.

Arising From the Space of 'Yes'

Connecting to the previous chapters, we can say that unconditional love arises spontaneously as a by-product of being in the space of 'yes'. Immediately, a difference to one of the most common uses of the word 'love' becomes apparent, since the word is often used to describe a state of desire: "I would love to be with her... I would love to be his girlfriend... I would love him to notice me..." and so on. Desire, as we have already seen, is future-oriented, arising from an inner attitude of 'no' towards the present moment, while 'yes' brings us into the present, and this shows that the word 'love' can indicate two polar opposite states – 'yes' and 'no' to what is happening now, in the present.

Unconditional love, in our use of the term, also differs from the love between a mother and her child, which is not a conscious decision on either side to love the other. At the root of mother-child love is a powerful bonding instinct, common to all mammals; nature's way of protecting the young and ensuring their survival, and therefore the continuation of a species. When said in this way, it doesn't sound very 'human' or elevated, and perhaps many mothers will object, but essentially this is how the mothering instinct functions.

The love between a man and a woman seems to arise more from choice and free will, but on the other hand we all know this state includes the experience of 'falling in love,' which can grip us so powerfully – pushing aside normal, rational behavior — that at times it seems as if we haven't freely chosen anything, but rather that nature and Dr. Fisher's neurochemicals have played some kind of trick on us. Nevertheless, romantic love can be an uplifting experience and can give us an energy boost and sense of freshness, innocence and wonder that perhaps no other experience in life is able to provide.

Even though there may be a strong biological component at work, especially in the beginning stages, we also experience in adult love partnerships a willingness to put aside our own personal preferences; in short, we are less governed by our ego structure. By being able to include another person in our heart, we may gain a glimpse of something beyond the limitations of our personality, and this expanded, open state may continue long after the dopamine levels have subsided.

Biological, Emotional, Psychological and Spiritual

Even within the same relationship what we mean by 'love' may depend on what level we are talking about. At a biological level, love relates to sex, sensuality and physical pleasure. At an emotional level, love means intimacy, trust and a feeling of closeness. At a psychological level, it means the sharing of common interests, such as enjoying a person's personality even when there is no physical attraction. On a spiritual level, love relates to the meeting of two beings beyond the personal, and here we may say that we love a person whose silence and presence touches us, feeling a deep sense of communion with this person. Each level of love relates to a certain need and when the need of one level is fulfilled, then usually the need of a higher level comes more to our awareness.

At the biological, emotional and psychological levels, love is a give and take relationship. We need something from the other and in return we give something back. So when we say "I love you' what we really mean is "I need something from you and in exchange I am ready to give something to you."

However, problems arise when wanting to receive becomes stronger, when more is needed from the other than we feel able to return. Then we start behaving like a needy child relating to a parent. So our need for the other has to be the need of an adult. Showing one's need may be difficult, but is also essential, because in such moments we become more truthful and are required to acknowledge the other person's importance to us. This acknowledgment makes us receptive and is often what helps the other person open towards us. Unless we are aware that we need something and are ready to expose this need, we cannot receive what we want.

However, it is also important to let ourselves feel what it is that we have to offer. In other words, in a balanced relationship as it exists between partners, we need to remember the give-and-take dynamic, so we do not behave like demanding children, but like adults, aware of both the need to receive and the ability to give.

Overflowing From Within

There is another level of love which is not fulfilled from outside, but more like an overflowing quality from within. Many mystics have talked about this quality of love and they describe it as compassion, as distinct from passion. Since it does not depend on the outside, nor on exchange, it is also beyond relationship, beyond biology and psychology. It is a side-effect of inner fulfillment.

We have momentary experiences of this state when we feel love for the other person irrespective of what he, or she, is doing. This is an immensely satisfying state to be in, since it gives us a taste of freedom as an intrinsic dimension of love, something we do not usually experience in our romantic affairs, which, on the contrary, often make us feel dependant on the other person.

In order to avoid confusion, misunderstanding and disappointment, it is important to be clear about the level of love we are experiencing. For example, as spiritual seekers, it is easy to be confused between what is our potential for love, in terms of feeling compassion and freedom, and what is our down-to-earth reality. This can lead to a denial, or suppression, of our ordinary human needs.

In other words, pretending to be holy and non-attached when your partner is flirting with someone else doesn't necessarily make you a better or more loving person. Desires are not to be transcended by effort of will, nor by idealism and wishful thinking. Transformation is a byproduct of accepting everything as it is, so our need for love is natural and has to be accepted and lived in a conscious way.

Meditation does not mean to withdraw from the challenge of love affairs, but to use the awareness kindled by meditation to see oneself more clearly in the mirror of relationship. In this way, we come to a deeper understanding of love itself and we may have the experience that love does not come from outside, but arises within.

The problem facing almost every human being is that we are usually so focused on the other person that we are convinced that he, or she, is the source of the love we feel and need. Unless we have an experience of unmotivated love, we will always think this way, remaining dependent on the other. And this is really one of the main reasons why therapy works: it is the unmotivated love of the therapist, when he does not want anything from the client that is so healing.

Common Misunderstandings about Love

Love needs to be accompanied by awareness, because in itself it is a blind force that moves us without any inherent consciousness of its own. Such a love cannot lead to deeper fulfillment. On the contrary, love can be one of the main reasons for our suffering and, when it is upside down, even turn into hatred. But the real problem is not love; it is unawareness.

Healing work in a therapy session often consists of helping a person deepen his understanding about love, so let's examine some of the misunderstandings that are part of our common experience.

1. A person feels that, because he loves someone, he should do something for the other in terms of relieving this person of a burden, or difficulty, as if love is a kind of duty, or charity. In reality, this is an interference in the other's person's life and

thus contrary to love, since it does not respect inter-personal boundaries.

Example: One partner is sick at home and the other feels guilty because he, or she, wants to go out dancing. If the healthy partner stays home, he feels resentful and trapped; if he goes out, he feels selfish and guilty.

2. A person feels that because he loves someone, he has a right to demand something from the other partner, as if saying "I love you" means that the other owes something to him. This is contrary to love, as it takes away the other's freedom.

   Example: A woman says to her husband that, if he loves her, he will not go away on a certain business trip. Rather, he should prove his love by staying home.

3. A person talks about love, when in reality he is trying to manipulate the other person in order to get what he wants.

   Example: The classic case, which we all know, is of a man trying to convince a woman to have sex with him by saying how much he loves her.

4. A person exaggerates his need to be loved and does not see how much he is loved already.

   Example: Shakespeare's tragic hero, Othello, who does not see how much his wife, Desdemona, loves him.

5. A person believes that love can only come from a particular partner.

   Example: This is one of the main reasons why people remain in unloving relationships for so long and do not feel motivated to move out of them.

6. A person may deny his or her need for love. This pretension usually covers an underlying need for love; beneath the anti-dependent facade this person is afraid to expose his need to others, maybe even to himself.

   Example: Almost all 'bachelor' or 'playboy' types of single men fall into this category.

7. A person may deny his own ability to be loving and may

exaggerate the other's potential. Behind this attitude, there may be a strong desire to stay together and a denial of one's own ability to be alone and fulfilled.

Example: A woman believes that if she loses her partner, she will lose all love, but then realizes that, in reality, she feels more love from other people than from her partner.

As can be seen from the above examples, one can mistake one's own prejudices for love, or one can blindly believe what the other says. When it comes to being loved, we often believe what someone says more than our own perception of reality, and this shows how desperate we are to be loved, even if it is only through hearing the words "I love you." On the other hand, when there is a real moment of love, we may not be ready to receive it, rejecting the other by saying that this love is not true.

These are just some examples of common misunderstandings that frequently arise in therapeutic sessions.

Conditioning Starts in Childhood

Conditioning about love starts in early childhood. It has its roots in the need of a child to receive nourishment, protection and loving support from his parents; it is a general human condition and part of nature. At the roots of love there is dependency, the dependency of a child on his mother. What is natural in the beginning becomes unnatural when it is expanded beyond the time-span of biological necessity.

In the normal, healthy course of events, a child begins in a state of helplessness and dependence, then slowly, as he grows up, becomes more and more independent from the mother. For this to happen, both mother and child have to agree to moving apart. In other words, what was one in the beginning has to become two — this is the flow of life.

From a higher perspective, it can be said that in life no one really becomes totally independent. Rather, in human society, we all live in a state of inter-dependence with each other, neither isolated and alone, nor clinging and glued to one another, but maintaining a healthy balance between these two polarities.

However, in terms of child development, problems begin when the parent, or child, or perhaps both, try in some way to prevent the natural process of moving apart. Instead, they start manipulating each other in different, but powerful ways. In the beginning, it is the parents who have more power to manipulate and exploit a child's needs and modern psychological literature is full of what is termed 'Early Life Conditioning' that focuses on this phenomenon.

"Mummy won't love you unless you clean up your room… Mummy doesn't love little boys who leave their muddy boots on the carpet…" and so on.

Soon, the child also learns the trick and will try to manipulate his parents in order to get what he feels he needs. In this situation, love is often used like a commodity to get what one wants from the other, which is far from its real meaning. It is also perceived as something that is within our control, as if it can be given, withheld, taken away, or lost.

Questioning Deep-Rooted Attitudes

These early experiences settle deep in the child's psyche and set the stage for our adult love relationships. Even when, in reality, we are no more dependent, we behave as if we are, and we manipulate each other in the same ways that our parents did to us, or as we did towards our parents: we threaten to deprive the other of our love, we demand to be loved out of a sense of entitlement, we ask questions like "Whom do you love more…?" Many other strange things happen in the name of love, but we rarely question these deep-rooted attitudes and behavior patterns.

Our learning as adults will be to question old concepts of love and gain new awareness and insight. For example, in a deeper sense, love can be neither given nor withheld; it can be only present or absent. It is not really in our control. It is a quality, not a quantity, and therefore cannot be more nor less.

Moreover, it does not really come from outside, nor from another person, but from within our own heart. At the most, the other may serve as a trigger or catalytic agent for the experience. It is as if the other is reminding us about something we had forgotten. But essentially love is a spontaneous phenomenon. It is not our choice, or decision. It comes from beyond us.

Mystics have been saying that love is the force that holds the universe together. Maybe that is the reason why, when we are genuinely touched by love, we feel humble and in a state of wonder, as if some universal force is moving through us. This may also be the reason why we cannot control it, secure it, direct it, or make promises about it.

One aspect that becomes apparent through deepening our understanding is that love and relationship are two different phenomena. They can happen together, but do not necessarily do so. Love, when accompanied by awareness, may eventually give an experience of something that is far beyond any relationship.

In the following chapters we examine the dynamics of relationship, how love operates within it, how suffering is the consequence of misunderstanding, and how conscious love can eventually lead to healing and fulfillment.

Chapter Six

Primal Relationship

When we speak of a 'primal relationship' we usually refer to the relationship between children and their parents, but it can also include other forms of relationship in which a 'superior' force is trying to regulate an 'inferior' one. Within our own bodies, for example, there is a primal relationship between the lower and higher energy centers. If there is conflict between these energy centers, it usually means that an energy from a lower center is trying to express itself, while another energy from a higher center is trying to stop or inhibit this expression.

We usually refer to this internal dynamic as the 'suppression' of our natural impulses. It is experienced by the individual as a conflict between what his natural impulses are urging him to do and what he feels he 'should' be doing; these 'shoulds' come from his childhood conditioning and include the values and beliefs picked up from his social environment. Such conflict often results in physical tension in the form of chronic holding patterns in the body's muscles and fascia, and is sometimes referred to as an 'energy block.' However, it is easier to see the problem in terms of movement: one energy is moving upwards and outwards, seeking expression and release, while the other energy is pushing downwards and inwards, seeking to stop the other movement. Inevitably, there is tension between them and a split occurs in the wholeness of an individual's energy.

This inner tension is mirrored in the conflict a child feels with his parents, teachers, or any kind of authority figure. He wants to act in a certain way and feels he is not being allowed to do so; in fact, he feels inhibited and condemned by them. He feels 'small,' like a child, and he sees the other as a 'big,' superior, adult, suppressive force.

A Freeing-up Process

As we saw in chapter two, the structure of the human brain mirrors this division, with the reptilian and mammalian areas representing the more basic impulses, while the neo-cortex represents more recently developed and more sophisticated intellectual processes. We also saw how the attempt to override lower impulses creates unresolved traumatic imprints, and one of the functions of therapy is to help people heal and integrate these, allowing frozen natural impulses to find some kind of completion.

This 'freeing-up' process is experienced by the client as an expansion and widening of life experience and can give a feeling of deep satisfaction. In order for this to happen, the natural impulses need to find expression and the therapist usually supports them against that which obstructs them. This is the classical approach of many therapeutic techniques. In this context, feelings of anger are seen as useful and necessary energies that empower the individual, and their expression receives encouragement from the therapist. However, as we will shortly see, this alone will not lead to a real resolution.

The Evolution of a Child

If one looks at a child's evolution one can see that the first stage has to do with assimilation and receiving from the parents. In the mother's womb and after birth a child mainly eats and sleeps. During this time, he is receiving nourishment and absorbing it unconditionally; if he would refuse, he would die. Assimilation is an essential evolutionary process and means that one digests what one receives, so it becomes part of one's own body and energy field.

In the beginning, a child cannot distinguish between himself and his mother, and does not understand the word 'I.' After reaching a certain maturity, however, he starts establishing and experimenting with his personal boundaries and, in order to do this, he needs to learn to say 'no.' Saying 'no' means that he is separating himself from others, especially from the mother. Now he learns to say 'me, not you,' creating a separate identity.

When children reach this stage they start saying 'no' to everything, even to things that are in their favor, just because they are experimenting with setting boundaries. This process also includes becoming aware of the boundaries of others, so it is important that the mother is clear about her own boundaries and can communicate this to her child.

This is a big subject in developmental psychology, but what is important in terms of a general understanding of the primary relationship is to know the basic stages: the initial unconditional 'yes' to the mother, and then the 'no' that allows the child to develop his own independence and strength.

When the child grows further, he will learn to say 'yes' or 'no' as a response to his own inner needs, not as a fixed pattern. He will be able to interact with the surrounding social environment, which requires a dialogue between his own inner impulses and those of other people. The child learns that sometimes his needs can be fulfilled, sometimes not, sometimes in a modified form, or at a later moment. Now he becomes capable of relating to others, finding bridges between what he needs and what others need.

This is the essence of childhood development, which psychology can expand on in many ways.

The Camel, the Lion, the Child

Friedrich Nietzsche, the nineteenth-century German philosopher, created a colorful metaphor for these three stages of 'yes,' 'no,' and 'yes or no,' applying it to the consciousness of adults. He called it the Camel, the Lion and the Child.

When we look at relationship patterns that reflect a primary relationship we see that there is usually one person saying 'you should' to another person, in either an obvious or more subtle way. There is a certain demand, expectation or pressure coming from one person to another. One is telling the other how to behave, act, think, feel... and so on.

The Camel: 'Yes' to the Other

The person on the receiving end may react in different ways and the first and simplest is described by Nietzsche as the 'camel' pattern. In this pattern, one basically says 'yes' to the demand, one becomes like a follower, or pleaser, and does one's best to fulfill the other's expectations. This is what most people do in life; they go along with what they have been told to do by others; by their parents, teachers, bosses, priests... by society in general. They want to avoid any conflict and would rather be unhappy than risk any conflict or fight.

The basic desire behind the camel's attitude is the desire to be loved, acknowledged, accepted, rewarded. It is also motivated by a fear of being isolated, ostracized and left alone. Even though real love doesn't come this way, the camel remains content with the small amount of attention he gets, even if it is negative in nature. In reality, the other doesn't really love or respect the camel. The more one remains in the space of the camel, the less is the possibility for authentic love to happen, but one remains hoping and dreaming of better times ahead.

On an energy level, camels eventually become tired, because of their continuous effort to fulfill the demands of others and their refusal to listen to their own inner impulses and needs. Physically, they often appear to be collapsed, with low energy. Typically, they will say sentences like "I do my best," or "please tell me how..." or "thank you for telling me what to do..." or "I can't make it by myself".

The pattern is named after the camel because this animal is used as a beast of burden and can endure hardships such as walking steadily through deserts for long distances without water. A person with this pattern denies that he has any real power and may see himself without any choice, essentially a victim, at the command of others.

The following example comes from a session with a woman who felt trapped in a camel pattern with her elder sister. In a gestalt dialogue between the two, this conversation took place:

Elder Sister: I feel so bad... and you are responsible for it.
Client does not answer, but looks miserable, heavy and collapsed.
Elder Sister: It's your fault that I'm in such a difficult situation.
Client: You know I love you and I want you to feel better. What can I do for you?
Elder Sister: You can at least make up for the damage that you did... and also apologize.
Client: I'm really sorry and will try my best to mend whatever is possible.
Elder Sister: Never do something like that to me again.
Client: I promise.

The Lion: 'No' to the Other

After having been in this pattern for a while, however, there may come a point when we feel we've had enough. Just like a child who develops from the first stage of saying 'yes,' we begin to explore saying 'no.'

Sometimes in relationship, after trying to be nice, doing what the other wants, yet still not experiencing the desired appreciation or love, we explode and express our frustration, telling the other person to go to hell. We rebel. This can also become a habit pattern, so that instead of automatically saying 'yes' to the demands of others, our first response is to say 'no.'

This is what Nietszche calls the 'lion' pattern. Symbolically, the lion stands alone, outside the crowd and consensus of public opinion. He fights, roars his defiance, defends his territory and does not allow others to intrude into his personal space without prior invitation. While the camel says 'You are right and I am wrong', the lion says 'I am right and you are wrong'. Other typical lion sentences include 'This is my life,' 'I do what I want,' 'Leave me alone,' or he attacks the other, saying, "Why don't you mind your own business?"

In terms of physical appearance, lions often appear to be rigid, as if holding themselves together, and usually store a lot of energy and tension in the body's extremities – hands, feet, arms – because they are ready at any moment to fight, to defend themselves, or to attack the other.

However, the lion is also trapped in a fixed behavior pattern and is not free to make a real choice between 'yes' and 'no' that is appropriate to the situation. He also makes himself dependent on others; whatever they want, demand or need, he takes the opposite position. He can also be manipulated, because he is predictable. For example, parents who know that their child will react with a 'no' can simply tell him to do the opposite of what they really want him to do. So a lion lives in the illusion of being free, just as the camel lives in the illusion of being powerless.

The following example is taken from a session with a female client who has developed the habit of being in the lion role towards her mother:

Mother: *You always do what you want. You're too wild… you should be*
*   more considerate of others. What will become of you?*
(The daughter takes a deep breath to show her irritation, tosses her hair
*   demonstratively and turns away).*
Daughter: *Nag, nag, nag…*
Mother: *And look at you hair, you should keep it more tidy.*
Daughter: *I like it exactly the way it is.*
Mother: *You don't care about others… you don't even listen.*
Daughter *(pretending not to listen and turning away even further): It's*
*   your problem, mom. Why don't you leave me alone?*

Often, the desire behind the lion pattern is a desire for freedom, or to be independent and without needs. But beneath the surface, the opposite reality is concealed. Lions remain in bondage to those whom they reject. Often, underneath the lion, a camel is hiding, something that can become painfully clear when we angrily tell our lover to 'get lost' and then he, or she, really leaves:

Woman: We need communicate more. The way things are, our relationship can't improve.

Man: But I told you what I feel… and right now I need to finish this repair job.

Woman: Our relationship isn't important to you; you put more energy into that damned motorbike.

Man: Nonsense. We just spent the whole weekend together.

Woman: But when problems come up, you always escape into work and don't want to talk.

Man: Look, stop nagging me. I can't stand this.

Woman: Well, if you can't stand me, I may as well leave.

She turns to leave the garage.

Man: Honey, wait… okay… what do you want to talk about? (lion collapses and camel appears)

Even though we have a predominant pattern in our relating, we often switch from the camel to the lion and vice versa. It is important to understand that both the camel and the lion need someone other than themselves to tell them what to do; the camel so he can follow and the lion so he can resist. One cannot be a camel or lion alone; the other functions as a projection screen and is given all the power in the relationship. But the real power lies with the camel or lion character, the one who is talking about himself and not the one who is saying 'you should.' The reason is clear: the person who says 'I' can change; rather than listening to the other, he can start to listen to himself. The moment a camel or lion decides to look in, rather than expecting love to come from someone else, a new possibility opens up.

The Child: 'Yes' to Oneself

When we drop the idea of finding fulfillment outside ourselves and realize that we are free to respond according to the requirements of the situation, we can move beyond the camel-lion paradigm. This third alternative is what Nietszche describes as 'the child,' not in the sense of being immature like a child, but in the sense of being innocent, spontaneous and natural, without preconceived ideas and attitudes. It is similar to the practice of saying 'yes to the moment' and allowing things to happen, as discussed in chapter two, but now the situation involves other people.

While the camel says 'yes' to the other and the lion says 'no' to the other, the child changes the whole gestalt and starts saying 'yes' to himself. The focus is no more on the other person, but on honoring the truth of his own being, which manifests as a creative response to the situation, independently of what the other wants. The child neither follows, nor resists the other, but remains open and flexible. He is ready to relate when the other is available, and ready to remain alone when the other is busy with desires.

Of these three roles, it is easiest to be a camel and most people remain habitually stuck in this pattern because it is safe and requires no intelligence; one can simply follow what someone else commands or advises. It is tiring and will not make anyone blissful, but it is safe and at least one is not alone.

To be a lion is more risky, since it tends to create conflict and a state of continuous tension and negativity. The nature of the lion's roar gives an upsurge of energy and one may have the illusion of being free and independent, but this may also mean that one remains without intimacy and love.

Real freedom comes not from saying 'no' to the other, but from saying 'yes' to oneself; it is a positive freedom, not freedom 'from,' but freedom 'for.' So the child may do what others say, or not do it; it is not a fixed, pre-determined response but comes from his inner 'yes' to himself; he remains independent and vulnerable at the same time.

Working with Patterns in Therapy

These relating patterns happen not only between two people, but within one person. We are often aware of inner voices that command us to 'do this' and 'don't do that,' and this is because the voices of people from our past, who told us how we should behave, have become internalized. We learned the values of our social surroundings to such a degree that we believe these voices to be our own, and cannot distinguish them from our own voice.

In therapy, a client usually receives support to identify his own inner voice and rebel against the 'shoulds' from other voices. The client is moving from being a camel to being a lion and many times the therapy ends at this point. However, if a therapist knows meditation, then he knows that real freedom comes from saying 'yes', not from saying 'no'. Then he supports his client to enter the space of the child.

The art of this approach is that the therapist has no desire for his client to be different. The moment he wants his client *not* to be a camel or a lion, he has become one of those voices that is saying 'you should.' Then the client may follow the therapist's advice and scream 'no' at his parents, or express his feelings, not because it is his own understanding and need to do so, but because it is expected of him. He knows how to please the therapist.

The art of being a therapist is to allow the client to remain as he is, without wanting anything from him. It is an invitation to enter the dimension of the child — more will be said about this subtle difference in chapter nine. For a client this is a real gift. It is a rare experience to be with someone who does not want anything from you, and I will talk about this more in chapter twelve.

Gestalt Role-Playing

A simple and effective way of working with these patterns is through the Gestalt process developed by German-born psychotherapist Fritz Perls, who gained international recognition for his technique in the 1960s. Now the basic principles of his method are used in therapy all over the world. The key to Perls' method is an understanding that what we react to in the other is often a reflection, or part, of ourselves.

In our use of Gestalt, two cushions are required, one for the dominating figure, the other for the person who is reacting to being dominated. The client begins in an 'observer' position, sitting facing the therapist with the cushions placed on either side, one on the client's left and the other on his right. The client is then asked to sit on one of the cushions and 'become' this character, then talk to the other character, in a role-playing exercise. On one cushion he plays himself, on the opposite cushion he plays 'the other'. In this way, he moves from cushion to cushion, changing roles and exploring the relationship between the two characters until the pattern becomes apparent.

When the client sits in the neutral, or observer, position he can look at what is going on in the relationship, together with the therapist. So, at times he role-plays the relating pattern, moving from cushion to cushion, while at other times he steps out of it and observes it.

The work of the therapist is to help the client become aware of which character is saying 'you should' and which side is reacting as a camel or a lion, and then help the client come out from reaction, establishing more self-connection. This means that the client is invited to look at his own feelings and explore the question 'what do I want?' irrespective of what the authority figure tells him to do. The answer comes from the space of the child, from an inner 'yes' to himself.

Intrinsically, we always have this freedom to look in. It is not an outer freedom that can be given, or taken away, but an inner freedom that nobody else can touch.

Coming Out of the Camel

Now it will be useful to return to the first example given in this chapter, in which an elder sister was dominating a client and pressuring her to apologize, which, entering the role of the camel, she willingly did...

Therapist to client: Is your sister happy now that you have apologized?
Client: No, not really. She's still not happy.
Therapist: I don't think it's possible that you can make her happy.
Client: I feel that's true.
Therapist: But can you see how you're trying to do that?
Client: Yes.
Therapist: And all that happens is that two people become unhappy instead of only one.
Client: Yes, I feel responsible for her.
Therapist: Can you see how you interfere in her freedom when you do that? And, in fact, with no good result. Love means you remain free and the other remains free as well. Can you imagine taking responsibility only for your own happiness?
The client starts relaxing, takes a deep breath and smiles in relief. She is beginning to understand how much of a burden she has been carrying by trying to take responsibility for her sister. Now she is entering the space of the 'child'.
After a while, she is invited to explore how she would respond to her sister with this new understanding, to see if she can maintain her own space while being pressured.
First, the client moves to the sister's cushion.
Elder Sister: It's your fault... you shouldn't have done that.
Then she moves to her own cushion and, in response, she chooses not to say anything, but continues to smile and this time does not take her sister's complaining attitude personally.
Now the client moves back to being her sister, who is still unhappy, but slightly more relaxed and less complaining than before.
In the work that follows, the client notices that her desire to receive love

from her sister is actually causing more tension for her sister. She wanted to make her sister happy in order to receive more love herself — demanding something which her sister was not capable of giving. Pleasing her sister was of no help, but not wanting anything from the sister was not only relaxing for her, but was also better for her sister. Her happiness was in her own hands. She understood that the real gift we can give to someone we love is our own happiness. Becoming aware of her body and her breathing proved a useful method of staying centered in herself, which helped her to come out of the pattern.

Coming Out of the Lion

In the second example, the client was stuck in the role of a lion when dealing with her mother's demands:

Therapist: How do you feel when your mother talks to you in this way?
At first, the client maintains her position of defiance and indifference.
Client: It's her problem, not mine. I'm fine as I am.
The therapist invites a deeper response by repeating the question.
Therapist: Yes, but how is it for you to be pressured in this way?
Now the client begins to inquire into her feelings.
Client: I feel cornered, caged in. My instinct is to leave.
Therapist: So, really, you are dependent on your mother's attitude. If she
   talks to you in this way, you feel you have to leave her house.
The client nods.
Therapist: Do you see any other possibility, other than leaving?
The client hesitates, then shrugs.
Client: I don't know.
The therapist invites the client to become aware of her body and her
   breathing.
Client: My god, I'm so tense... I didn't even know how tense this thing
   with my mother is making me.
The client changes her position, starts to breathe more deeply and keeps
   moving in order to reconnect with her body and allow some of the

tension to discharge. After a while, she starts to relax, then smiles. She has begun to come back to herself. All this work happened on the cushion representing the client. Now she is asked to shift to the other cushion and act as her mother.

Mother: I like my daughter.

Client moves back to her own place.

Client: This makes me happy. Now I can't leave, I have to stay.

The client has lost her connection to herself and becomes a camel, because of her need to be loved by her mother.

Therapist: To me, this sounds strange. A moment ago, your mother was not happy with you... now she says she loves you. It sounds like another way of manipulating you. Before, you said, "I have to leave." Now you say, "I can't leave." But really you are in the same cage. Can you see any other choice?

Client: It's my feeling that I can't leave.

Therapist: Yes, but is it true? Examine your feelings more deeply, because they are also conditioned by others.

The client sits for a while, reflecting, tuning in to her body.

The client has been sitting with her arms wrapped around her legs and her knees pulled up to her chin, in a defensive position, looking like a defiant little school girl. Now she relaxes and opens up her body position. Slowly, she comes out of being a camel and spontaneously starts laughing at herself.

Client (still smiling at herself): No, I can leave.

Being non-serious is often a significant first step in entering the space of the child. In the continuation of the session the therapist helps the client explore new possibilities how to respond to her mother from a non-serious space, which eventually deprives the mother of energy to continue to control.

Lion Hiding Camel

In the following example, we see a camel hiding beneath the role of a lion, which is a common form of behavior in many kinds of relationships. Here, the client is exploring her relationship with her father, playing both roles in a gestalt exchange:

Father: I want you to play the violin.

Client: I want to watch TV.

Father: That really hurts me.

Client: I know.

Therapist: What happens to you when your father talks like that?

Client: I feel pressurized and get angry.

Therapist: What else do you notice when you are pressured by him?

In response, the client starts crying and stops being a lion, entering the space of a camel.

Client: It makes me afraid.

The client looks at the therapist with tear-stained eyes, asking for help.

Therapist: Can you see how you are trying to manipulate me with your tears?

The client stops crying and after a few minutes becomes more calm.

Therapist: How are you actually feeling?

Client: Not so bad, but shaky.

Therapist: Is it okay to be a bit shaky?

Client: Yes.

The therapist removes the 'father' cushion for a moment.

Therapist: How is it now, when your father is not here?

Client: I miss him.

Therapist: So it seems you really want your father to love you. But maybe he does not have the capacity for the kind of love you seek. Maybe he can't fulfill your demands. But I think you can get love in other ways from other people. Do you have any experience of this?

The client smiles and brightens up.

Client: Yes, of course.

The client talks about different ways in which she feels loved in her life.

The therapist brings back the 'father' cushion.

Therapist: How does it feel now, when your father asks you to play the violin and you are not in need of his love?

Client: This is very new... I need time to feel this.

The session continued.

The Change of Dimension

In these examples, we see how our conditioning gives us the idea that love has to come from a particular person and, if it does not, then we feel lost. This keeps us in tension, fear, hopes and dreams. It creates bondage, not only for ourselves, but also for the person to whom we are relating. A person who insistently hopes to receive love from another is sure to find someone who has a similar desire and the relationship will soon fall into a fixed pattern and eventually create misery for both.

The learning is that we can be nourished in many ways, by many people and eventually come to realize that love springs from within our own inner being. This is the shift into another dimension, the space of the child, the dimension of conscious and spontaneous response with no future dreams. Now one is related to oneself. If the other, even only for a single moment, also enters this dimension, the relatedness will have a totally different quality. It will not be stuck in a certain pattern; instead, there will be a feeling of mutual respect for individual freedom, while at the same time experiencing a deeper sense of union than can be known as a camel or lion.

The challenge in our relationships is to examine if the motivation for our actions comes from within, or from outside ourselves. Are we saying 'yes' to ourselves? Or are we in some kind of reaction, hoping to be appreciated and loved by others? This is the potential learning in all our relationships.

Chapter Seven

Man-Woman Relationship

When we look at the relationship between a man and a woman, we are looking at a dynamic connection between two equals in which no one is lower and no one is higher, where intrinsically there is balance. Problems arise as a result of a disturbance of this balance, for example, when one partner tries to dominate the other and take more control or power than is appropriate.

When we look at the difference between the primal patterns discussed in the previous chapter and those that develop between a man and a woman, the main difference is that now the other is not just a projection with no reality of his own. When we investigated the camel and lion patterns we saw that the other is needed as a projection and once a person evolves to the level of consciousness known as the child he comes out of desire and therefore out of bondage. The authority character who was saying 'you should' loses all importance and reality.

However, in a relationship between a man and a woman the situation is usually not like that. The other does not disappear when one becomes more connected to oneself. So in addition to the patterns described in chapter six, there can be two more possibilities: both sides can say 'I want,' or one can say 'I want' while the other says 'I don't want.' They can have the same desire or they can be in conflict when their desires differ.

Two Kinds of Love
We saw before that there are two kinds of happiness, one that depends on getting what we want and another that does not depend on the outside, but comes from within, from being connected to oneself. In a similar way, a man and woman in

relationship can experience two kinds of love: they can be 'in love' because they have the same desires, the same interests, such as a shared sexual attraction, or a shared social ambition, and if their happiness depends wholly on this kind of bond then it is likely to be short-lived. We all know how quickly desires can change, because the human mind is continuously in a restless flux: one day it wants this, another day something else.

Many relationships are forged in this way, with people changing partners in the same way that they change houses or jobs, because the mind needs new forms of stimulation, otherwise it gets bored. It pursues excitement, but never finds real fulfillment. So, usually, the satisfaction in these kinds of relationships lasts for a short time only and is followed by boredom or disappointment when the partners start seeing that the other may not give them the fulfillment for which they had hoped.

The other way of 'being in love' is more a happening than the result of desire. It comes from being connected to oneself and because the other is also connected in the same way there is a certain expansion in one's joyfulness, as if two 'happinesses' become one. This kind of love does not come from effort, or wanting anything, but, on the contrary, arises suddenly and spontaneously. It may last only a short while, or it may continue, but either way it is deeply fulfilling. Many poets and mystics have talked about this kind of love as a spring breeze that comes and goes on its own accord. It is not in our hands to make it happen, nor is it in our hands to keep or prolong it.

A Working Agreement

So these are the two kinds of relationship: one where a connection between the partners depends on desire and the other where both already have a certain inner fulfillment before they meet. In the first case, the couple usually begins in a state of happiness, commonly known as the 'honeymoon' phase, and this is gradually replaced by a state of compromise, which develops as the honeymoon period ends. Compromise is the result of 'coming back to earth,' acknowledging the other's ordinariness, realizing that expectations were too high and negotiating a working agreement or contract – either spoken or unspoken. This is the 'teamwork' phase when a couple may agree to enter into a long term relationship out of a desire for companionship, a fear of being alone, and pressure from social voices – both internal and external — to 'settle down' and do what everyone else is doing.

When the compromise wears thin, yielding too little in terms of warmth, love, tenderness or mutual support, one or both of the partners may look to therapy as a way of resolving situations in which there is too much conflict. But rather than looking in, the partners often remain in the state of trying to get from each other what they think they need in order to be happy. So they remain in continuous tension, because even if they get something from the other, they have to be careful to maintain the agreement and not break it. This model of relating is common in our society, with two people somehow glued together, trying to be happy and trying to avoid pain, but the underlying tension and effort remains.

Many times, couple therapy operates on this level and rather than helping the two partners find fulfillment, they are taught how to create a modified or renegotiated compromise with each other; in other words, to accept a state in which they are not too happy and not too miserable. This helps to a certain degree and is accepted as a necessary part of human relationships, but on the other hand it excludes the immense potential of every human being to find fulfillment and wholeness within himself.

Unfortunately, most people have no idea that finding an inner source of well-being offers a genuine solution to the seemingly endless and ultimately fruitless task of trying to find permanent fulfillment through someone else. The aim of spiritual therapy is not just to help people learn how to remain together and fulfill their desires through a partner, but to help each individual find an inner fulfillment that does not depend on the other's presence or absence. This would automatically ease tensions within the relationship.

Accepting Dual Experiences

On the level of the mind and its desires, we operate in a world that almost always presents us with dual experiences: we know happiness, but we also know that unhappiness follows it like a shadow; we know love, but we also know the emptiness, loneliness, pain, bitterness or anger that comes when love has gone. A wise person does not fight for one side of this duality and try to deny the other, but accepts both as part of the flow of life, and as a consequence of how the human mind functions.

Ups and downs follow each other as regularly as waves in the ocean. If we can accept this deeply, we enter another dimension that is beyond the duality of the mind, realizing that only in the inner world is it possible to experience a state of continuous fulfillment.

Sometimes we have glimpses of this state, for example, when we unexpectedly experience an inner peace during a 'down-swing' period in our lives when, on the outside, things seem to be falling apart. A relationship breaks up... a business project doesn't work out... yet, curiously, we feel calm and at ease. For example, Aldous Huxley, the English author, reported that, late in his life, when his house in California burned down with all his possessions inside, the only emotions he felt were immense relief and inner calm.

Sometimes, just like Huxley's experience, these things happen by themselves, spontaneously arising from within, but meditation is the only method that teaches this state as a base-line for day-to-day living.

Men Are From Mars...

In the early 1990s a book called *'Men Are From Mars, Women Are From Venus'* by John Gray became an international best-seller simply because it acknowledged the fact that men and women are different by nature, think and feel differently, and mean different things when they use the same language. From the perspective of counseling and therapy, it is important that men and women should be helped to recognize, accept and enjoy their differences, understanding that the dynamic movement between their opposing polarities brings joyful times of coming together, of melting and merging into oneness, and other times when no meeting is possible.

One of the lessons for partners is to retain a certain inner joyfulness, even when the other is unavailable. This includes respecting each other's differences and enjoying one's aloneness, which is possible only when one does not focus on the other person, on what we want, or do not want, from him or her.

Let's look at some practical examples of the male-female dynamic and see what can help to solve conflict. As described in the previous chapter, the client is invited to use the Gestalt method of exploration, placing himself alternately on two opposite cushions, one representing himself and one his partner. He enters a dialog, playing himself and his partner, talking from the partner position as if he is this partner, imagining how the partner would respond. He talks in the present tense, as if the dialog is happening now, in the moment.

Example 1: 'You Should'… 'I Don't Want'

The client is a man, who is examining the relationship with his partner:
Woman: You have to listen to me. I don't have space to share what I feel.
Man: But I have no space for you right now.
Woman: It's always like this. When I need to share, you don't have any space.
Man: But what can I do, it's like that now. I don't have space for you.
This kind of dialog can continue endlessly. The woman says 'You should' and the man reacts as a lion, saying 'I don't want.' Both have real feelings behind their desires, but because they are so focused on the

other person they do not enter their feelings and so no solution for their difficulty is possible in this state.

The therapist intervenes and talks to the man:

Therapist: What happens to you if the woman talks to you like this?

Man: I'm protecting myself.

Therapist: Yes, and how do you feel? Can you sense that?

Man: I feel tense.

He remains unmoving and looks stiff. The therapist asks him to move his body.

Man: I feel better… and I notice that I'm angry.

Therapist: Is it okay for you to feel that?

Man: No, it's not. I should be more gentle with a woman.

Therapist: Is this actually true?

Man (laughing): I don't think so. My father was often fighting with my mother and I don't want to be like him.

The man is in a lion pattern with his partner and he suppresses his anger, because of a conditioned belief that a man should not be angry with a woman. Before he can enter the child space, which means finding his own joyfulness, he would first need to allow the suppressed energy, the held-back desire, and allow himself to be angry and maybe enjoy the vitality that it brings.

On a psychological level, it is clear that the client rejects his father and tries to protect his mother. But because he does not want to be like his father and does not want to be angry, he unintentionally builds up more anger. Whatever we suppress gains strength and dominates us more.

Therapist: Sometimes it is a great feeling to be angry. It gives one power and strength.

Man (starting to enjoy and laugh): Yes, I like that.

For a while the therapist helps the client to explore his anger and how his body feels when he allows this energy, which gradually trans-forms into aliveness.

After shifting the client to the woman's cushion, the therapist asks 'her' how 'she' is doing.

Woman: He is always like this. No time for me.

Back on the man side.

Therapist: How are you when she complains about you?

Man's joy disappears and he collapses.

Man: I cannot do anything. I feel somehow guilty and insecure

The man's attention again went from feeling his own joy and physical strength to the woman. Because her approval is so important, his joy is lost. In further work on this issue, the therapist helps the client focus more on his own body, his breathing and what his body wants to do. He helps the client be aware not to fall into the collapsed state of the camel or the rigid state of the lion, which means not remaining stuck in anger. Gradually, the client starts to relax with his own insecurity and becomes vulnerable. He notices that he was more occupied with saying 'no' to the woman, or asking her permission, than actually finding out what he would enjoy to do.

Back to the woman:

Therapist: How do you feel now?

Woman: I feel I can relax now. I notice that I was really so afraid to lose contact with him.

When the woman can see that his decision to take space is not against her, she can also explore her own feelings. She was afraid to lose her partner; she was so focused on him that she could not look at her herself in a deeper way and was unaware of her fear. In the following Gestalt work, the client learns that the woman pressured him out of her fear and that he reacted to her, because he felt deep down responsible for her. After learning that love does not mean to take responsibility for someone else's feelings, but only for one's own state, he also discovers that he can accept her fear without trying to save her from it. Now he does not need to react as before. Staying in contact with himself also helps the woman to contact herself.

Unlike in the previous chapter, where one of the two figures was a projection with no reality behind it, here, both characters have their own individuality and their own feelings. Both need to find their connection to themselves, but usually one of the two has more capacity to do this than the other, and this is the character who will have to take the first step in finding self-connection. In this example, it was the man's side.

Example 2: Fear of Losing Love

Woman (addressing the cushion that represents her partner): I'm really angry with you. I feel manipulated.

She shifts to the man's cushion:

Man: I just do what I want.

Shifting back:

Woman: I'm so angry. I feel helpless when you are like this.

Talking to the therapist: It's a challenge for me to feel helpless and not blame my partner. I usually do blame him, but I also think it's good for me to feel the helplessness.

(It's already clear that the woman has ideas about what she 'should' do. She has done a lot of therapy already.)

Therapist: It is the same, whether you blame or feel helpless. In both cases you want him very much. Is he very important for you? What are you afraid to lose?

Woman: Intimacy and affection.

Therapist: Exactly, you are afraid to lose love. Let us examine, is it true that you will lose all love if he goes?

Woman: No.

Therapist: Feel where love is coming from right now.

The client talks about the people in her life who love her. She starts smiling.

Therapist: How do you feel now?

Woman: Better.

Therapist: Now look at the man. Maybe he cannot, or does not want to give you love. How is it, if you don't get love from him? Do you feel in any way different compared to before?

Woman: It's different. I feel better and not so helpless as before. Still I have a hope.

Therapist: Yes, hope can be dangerous. To build anything on hope usually results in misery. Let's look at this moment. Right now, he is not loving. It is okay to feel a bit sad, but to think you have lost all love is dangerous.

Again, the therapist invites the client to think of the people who love her, with whom she can connect and feel nourished or supported.

Therapist: So not everything is lost, if he doesn't love you.

Woman smiles and agrees. Now the client shifts to the cushion representing the man on whom she has been focusing.

Therapist: How are you? It looks as if she doesn't need you as much as before.

Man: Now I get angry.

Therapist: Yes, you are no more in control of the situation. What do you feel?

Man: I don't want her to go away.

This is a common situation between men and women. When one partner wants, the other says 'no,' but when wanting starts changing into not wanting, the other starts wanting. In this case, it appears that the man is more afraid and more dependant than the woman. He played the stronger one and she played the weaker one, while the reality is just the opposite.

Back to the woman.

Therapist: How do feel when he asks you not to go?

Woman: I feel I want to stay in my space. I also need something from him and he can't just do what he wants.

Now the woman reacts as lion. It is a typical situation between partners: the struggle for power, control and domination. Now she feels she has the power and wants to dictate her conditions, but she has lost her self-connection.

Therapist: This is called a contract: 'If I do something for you, then you need to do something for me.' This always ends in misery. It's clear that he is needy and cannot give much to you, so trying to force him won't help. Can you imagine responding to him from the openness and love you just felt a moment ago? Without feeling you need to do anything?

Woman: Yes, I don't want to do anything.

Now the conditioning on the woman side becomes clear. When it comes to love, she thinks she has to do something. But mothering the other is not really love; one controls the other by making oneself indispensable and reduces the other to a child.

In the following work, the woman learns to stay in a loving space without doing anything for the man. It also turns out that the man goes with other women, because he is not able to commit to her. He feels dependent on women, which frightens him and he does not want to feel his fear. For the woman, the challenge is to remain in a loving space without rejecting the man and without taking care of him. Before, she was taking everything personally and felt over-responsible, as if she is at fault, when in reality it is his incapacity to commit that is the real problem.

This is a good example of what we do in relationships: We take things too personally, as if things happen because of us, and this is a kind of weakness. Strength, on the other hand, lies in one's ability to be happy when alone. Real love arises out of this ability; it comes from aloneness. In the work, the therapist asks the more mature person to come out from desire and connect to her true capacity, which in turn removes a false sense of strength from the other character and brings him in contact with his true reality. Now further growth becomes possible.

Example 3: The Dream of a Perfect Partner

The client is the woman. She begins with the man side.

Man: You should communicate more...you're too silent. I don't know what you feel, I don't know what you think... and I feel you're hiding something.

Woman: I'm not hiding anything. I just feel that you cannot give me what I want, but I have nothing to speak about.

Man: Do you think you are spiritually enlightened or something? You look like you know everything.

The man side is very much into 'you.' We work more with the woman side because she is more connected to herself and therefore has more presence. What is her reaction to the man's accusations? She says 'no' — I am not hiding – so she reacts as a lion.

Therapist to the woman side: How do you feel when he talks to you like that?

Woman: I feel pressure, and I like to explain what's going on with me. But somehow it is like I am talking to a wall.

Therapist: So you want something from him; maybe that he understands you, or that he loves you, this is not happening. Are you disappointed? (Often a lion is deep down disappointed, anger often comes from disappointment).

Woman: Yeah... yes.

Therapist: Let yourself feel this, for a moment.

It is difficult for her to say what she really feels and this is typical for a lion position. The lion is so busy protecting herself, pretending not to need anything, that often she is not connected with what she really wants. So the lion, even by not speaking, gives a lot of energy to the other. One may just read a newspaper, but when it is a reaction, a 'no' to the other, it comes across loud and clear — the other can feel it.

Therapist: Let us start with the beginning, which means being human and having needs and desires. How is it for you to want something from a man? Can you feel that you want something? How is it to allow yourself that?

 Woman: It's difficult.

(The lion protects her vulnerability. Probably, there are past wounds and hurts.)

Therapist: Take a moment. If you can feel it right now, you can let me know — you don't have to tell the man. Can you tell me what you want from him?

The woman starts laughing, because now she realizes that she wants something. By allowing this, her energy expands, becomes lighter, more natural. Before she was quite heavy. It is important to take away

*all the judgments such as, for example, the idea that one should not
have desires. The woman starts laughing more.*

Therapist: *It's okay… even if you think it's a ridiculous desire. (More
laughter) It's great to be a bit ridiculous. So what is it?*

Woman: *I want a partner with whom I can really share, maybe have a
house and children. For me, relationship means to be able to trust
each other, to enjoy together…..*

*She keeps going for a while. What emerges is that she has a lot of ideas
and dreams about how relationships should be. When it doesn't
happen in this way with a man, such as now, the disappointment and
frustration sets in. However, it is important for her to feel the disappointment rather than pretending not to need anything. When she
laughed, she relaxed into being ordinary.*

*So, behind the lion's reaction, she has a big desire and the man reacts to
it. So, even though in the beginning it looked like the pressure was
coming from the man's side, the real pressure comes from the
woman's side, through her big expectations.*

Therapist: *Right now you are laughing, so it looks like you don't take it
so seriously.*

Woman: *Well… I can see… I expect a lot.*

Therapist: *Yes, but look at him right now. Obviously, he is not matching
your big expectations. How is that for you? How do you feel about
it?*

Woman keeps laughing about herself.

Therapist: *Look at him again. Obviously, you're not getting what you
want from him. He is not the perfect man to fulfill your desires, so
how is that for you?*

Woman becomes a little more serious.

*Looking at the other, the dream starts again, even though a moment
before nothing was missing. The moment the other comes in, one
loses self-connection.*

*The therapist helps the woman to be aware of this, and she connects with
herself again.*

Now the client changes to the man cushion.

Therapist to man: She has just discovered that she wants you to be
perfect. She discovered that she puts a lot of pressure on you and was
able to laugh about herself. So how you feel right now?
Man: I feel more relaxed.
The energy to attack the woman has subsided. It also means that his
attack was in reality a defense. The man went on to say that he felt
unloved and further work revealed that the client's challenge in this
situation is to remain loving, because she has this capacity when not
caught up in her desires. She needs to go beyond the lion, connecting
with her child space.

Who Is Stronger?

One of the main points in this kind of work is to decide who has
real strength and who has not. Strength is one's potential to be
present, even in a pressurized situation, and to remain in a loving
space. Usually, the problem is that the one who has real strength
believes the other to be stronger and does not take responsibility
for his or her own capacity. In other words, one character makes
himself or herself too small, while the other becomes too big. In
terms of working in a session, more can be expected from the
'strong' person, as he, or she, has more understanding and
awareness, while the 'weaker' side is allowed to remain closed —
one does not expect any change on this side. However, when one
character starts taking responsibility, the other is bound to be
affected: he can begin to relax and start to explore himself more
deeply.

In the previous case, for example, the woman decided to be
more present, less caught up in dreams of perfection, and then the
man could begin to relax and discover his need for love, rather
than remaining in reaction to the woman. Through relaxation into
this need, his own capacity for love may eventually start to grow,
which will make a deeper meeting possible in the future. Until
then, the woman needs to accept this 'imperfect' man without
desiring more — in other words, loving him as he is.

Guided Meditation to Understand Relating

Usually, in relating we want something from somebody, or somebody wants something from us. Here is a short exercise to experience how this can affect us.

Sit comfortably, in a quiet place where you will not be disturbed for 10-15 minutes.

Close your eyes.

Remember a situation in your life in which you wanted, or needed, something from someone else. Let the memory come back to you now. Take a few minutes to recall the feelings it generated in you.

Next, recall a situation in which someone wanted something from you. Stay with this remembrance for a few moments, focusing on this type of relationship and the feelings it evoked in you.

When you have completed both steps, let these memories go.

Now, think of any experience of love-relating in your life that happened not because you wanted something, but because the connection just happened; it came as a surprise. Just notice if you have ever experienced something like this.

When you have done this, let yourself come back to your body, your breathing: let your body be loose, your shoulders, your arms… your breathing is easy and relaxed. Find a space in yourself where you don't want anything right now. Nothing is missing.

Now imagine you are standing opposite a partner, who says to you "Please love me". Observe your inner reactions to this. Do you withdraw, or are you happy that someone wants something from you? What else do you notice?

In the same way observe your reaction to other statements: for example if the other says, "You are so beautiful," or to more negative statements like "You are not really open." With each statement, give time to observe your reaction. What sentences affect you most? Are you reacting as camel, or as lion?

Now let it all go and bring your attention back to yourself. Are you ready and capable to be happy on your own?

Acknowledging the Need for Each Other

Human relationships arise because we experience ourselves as incomplete. A man without a woman feels incomplete and so does a woman without a man. This creates relationship: we acknowledge that we need something from the other and this also shows that the other is valuable to us.

However, it is important not to confuse this adult need with a child who needs his mother's unconditional love and support. This distinction is of fundamental importance for having a successful and grown-up partnership, because it implies that each partner is aware that, to a certain extent, he can be fulfilled even without the other. He, or she, can enjoy aloneness. Togetherness will add to one's joy, but one does not wholly depend on it.

This understanding grows with meditation, where we learn to find fulfillment in aloneness, as we have been discussing in previous chapters. Eventually, there comes a point in the spiritual evolution of consciousness where the need for the other ceases completely — what is generally called 'Buddha consciousness.' Until then, we will depend on someone outside ourselves to find wholeness, admitting that this need is essential and natural. Anything else is simply pretension and a suppression of our natural life force.

When we look at the general tendencies in relationships, we see that a man is mostly afraid to lose his freedom and his ability to do what he wants, while a woman is mostly afraid to lose love, to lose the beloved as her object of love. So the learning for the man will be to understand that freedom is an inner quality that does not depend on the outside. The woman needs to understand that, essentially, love is an intrinsic human condition that cannot be lost, even when the partner goes; the other only provokes a quality that, in reality, is always present inside oneself.

For both men and women, this learning means they need to let go of old beliefs that are part of a wrong conditioning and examine what is actually true and what is untrue.

For example, when one is too afraid to lose the partner, or to lose the partner's love, one has in fact already lost it. What one can lose is not love, but something else... maybe security, maybe respect, maybe possessions. But love itself cannot be lost. It is therefore clear that many relationships are more like a business arrangement than an authentic, living love affair. When we really have a moment of love, all fear disappears. In fact, love and fear cannot co-exist, because they are opposites. Love gives courage, love means one trusts unconditionally. When one is in love, there is no fear.

Chapter Eight

Inner Male-Female Polarity

The Jungian school of psychology has developed the model of 'inner man' and 'inner woman,' something that has been acknowledged in both China and India since ancient times. Looking at the Taoist symbol of yin and yang, we see a deep understanding of opposing yet complementary forces at work in all aspects of nature: light and dark, summer and winter, male and female. Looking at the practices of Tantra, where the union of male and female energies is used to access higher states of consciousness, we find the same understanding. In both traditions, the outer meeting of male and female is reflected by an inner meeting, within the individual, and in modern times, Carl Gustav Jung, one of Sigmund Freud's most brilliant students, discovered the same truth.

Exploring the nature of the human psyche, Jung found that if the conscious part of the mind is that of a man then his unconscious is that of a woman; similarly, if the conscious part is female, her unconscious is male. If one thinks about it, it makes sense: each of us is born from the meeting of a man and a woman and our whole body, every cell of it, is a creation of this duality. The structure and function of the human brain also reflects the male-female meeting, being divided into right and left hemispheres. We refer to the right hemisphere as the 'feminine brain,' which is more responsible for intuition and governs the left side of the body; and we refer to the left hemisphere as the 'masculine brain,' which is more responsible for speech and logical decision-making and governs the right side of the body.

Inner Man, Inner Woman

So we can say that everyone has a male side and a female side. Of course, in terms of neurology and biology, the human organism is more complex, and we must keep in mind that this is only a 'working model' to understand ourselves better. We begin to use this model by imagining that in each person, whether man or woman, there is an 'inner man' and an 'inner woman.' It might be objected that, as a man, there is no 'inner man,' since the outer expression is already masculine; similarly, it can be argued that there is no 'inner woman' for a woman. But this is not the case. When a man begins to address his hidden female side this very process creates the understanding that there are two polarities, two energies, in a dynamic relationship within one individual. The same is true when a woman begins to explore her 'inner man;' it highlights her awareness of her female side as well.

So, for both sexes, we treat the 'inner man' and 'inner woman' as if they are two persons in relationship with each other, living in the same house, which is the physical body. Mostly, men tend to identify more with their male side while their female side is more hidden, whereas women usually identify more with their female side, while their male side remains more in the unconscious.

The Phenomenon of Projection

Outer love relationships can reflect the hidden polarity that is within us – mirroring outside what is concealed inside—and this is usually referred to as a 'projection.' One indication of a projection is that it holds a lot of energy, in a positive as well as in a negative sense, which is a psychological way of saying that we think the partner is either wonderful or we cannot stand him, or her. Either we are looking through rose-tinted spectacles or we don't want to look at all. In both cases, we are not aware that this same quality that we think to be so great or so terrible in the other person is actually something we are carrying inside ourselves. It is a disowned or denied aspect of our own psyche. So we do two things: first we 'project' it onto the other person, then we react to it in some way.

In other words, whatever we disown in ourselves is reflected back to us through other people with whom we are in relationship. This is one of the basic findings of psychoanalysis and constitutes part of almost every school of psychotherapy. This, too, is why we tend to get so attached to a particular outside partner. Our own inner male or inner female gets reflected back to us through the other and the more accurate this reflection is to the actual truth, the stronger the bond we experience with that person.

But we cannot just say that a man's outer woman mirrors his inner female side and a woman's outer man mirrors her male side. The situation is more complex. For example, it is also possible that the male side of the outer woman is reflecting some aspect of the man's own male qualities and this may provide the main motivating force for the bond between them. For a woman, the feminine side of her man may be reflecting an aspect of her inner woman. In fact, one can say that in one love relationship there are four people relating with each other: the two sides of each partner.

In our love relationships, the dynamic between our inner polarities is not fixed. We may experience that sometimes we are relating more from our male side and at other times more from our feminine side, and this can happen whether we are a man or a woman. Within a single relationship, we switch many times between the two sides, but usually there is one side that is dominant and this is sure to be reflected in some way in our outer partner.

As you can see, the inter-play between male and female energies in a love partnership can be a complex mix and one can easily become confused about who is relating with whom. In order to avoid a big muddle, we should keep in mind that the purpose of this investigation is to bring something that is hidden into the light of understanding. The model of inner male-female inter-action can bring clarity to issues we face in our relation-ships, as well as in other areas of our life, like work and creativity.

Projection: How it Works

To emphasize the main point: the more connected we feel to someone and the more we love someone, the more this person becomes our projection screen and when we understand this phenomenon the opportunity arises to see ourselves reflected in it. Through a partner, we see something about ourselves of which we are not directly aware, or at least not very clearly.

For example, I may feel that I am an independent and self-sufficient type of person, but in my relationships I usually meet a partner who seems needy and easily becomes dependent on me. In terms of projection, this is a clear indication that I am disowning my own feelings of need and fear, which I may have suppressed so deeply that I cannot feel them, but they come back to me through the mirror of the other. Or, I may believe that I am 'not the jealous type' and yet I seem to attract partners who are extremely possessive and jealous, watching my every move. Here, I am trying to place myself above the animal passions – perhaps for spiritual reasons – but the reality comes back to me through my partner.

However, it is not only our negative feelings that we disown, but positive feelings, too. For example, as a man, I may not be in touch with my own sensitivity and capacity for love, and yet I seem to attract partners who are extremely sensitive. It is the same phenomenon of projection; whatever polarity has been hidden can be seen reflected in the other and then contacted directly in oneself.

If we review the sample sessions from the previous chapter, it is clear that, when the client is sitting on the cushion of his partner, talking from there, he is not only playing his partner in an outer relationship, but in many aspects he is also expressing a hidden side of himself. Sometimes a client is aware of this fact, at other times he may lack this understanding, but as a therapist one has to keep in mind that almost all problems in relationships arise because of projection — because one or both partners cannot see in themselves what they find so disturbing in the other.

Owning the Hidden Sides

There is a great saying that in order to resolve a problem in a love relationship only one person needs to change, but this one person is always you. In other words, no problem can persist in a relationship unless you, as an individual, are in some way cooperating with it and supporting it. However, the problem is that almost everybody is looking at the faults in the other person and expecting the other to change, applying direct or indirect pressure to make such changes happen, or at least hoping that things will turn out better in the future.

As we saw in our previous discussion, hope and expectation are aspects of the desiring mind, which cannot say 'yes' to the present; therefore, anyone who remains in this state of demanding change from the other is sure to end up feeling tense and frustrated. In relationship, the solution for any problem comes when one is able to agree to the situation as it is now, which means to unconditionally accept the partner as he or she is. This acceptance can be greatly helped by discovering and owning hidden sides of oneself and by becoming aware of one's inner polarity of male and female energies.

There are different approaches through which the qualities of the inner man and the inner woman can be made conscious, for example, through energy readings, specific meditations and Gestalt dialogue. Another way is to examine an important relationship that you have experienced at some time in your adult life, as this person is likely to hold many qualities of your own inner man or woman.

Harmony and Disharmony

When people first become aware of their male-female polarity they naturally think they need to create harmony between their inner man and inner woman. After all, it is similar to wanting a harmonious relationship with an outer love partner. However, when we look more closely at this desire for harmony we find a subtle pressure or expectation directed toward the inner man or inner woman and again, through this new ideal, the desiring mind is creating a no-win situation. As with our outer partners, the inner man, or woman, is likely to react to such pressure in a defensive or hostile way.

It is important to learn to accept that conflict is part of any relationship, including the inner relationship, and that there is going to be a limit to how close and harmonious a man and woman can be at any particular moment in life. Nothing is achieved just by wanting to have harmony and balance. Inner development is a slow process that takes patience and an ability to relax with what is, without wanting an idealized union with the other.

However, relationship is one of the areas where our desires are strongest and, as we have seen in the previous chapter, one partner in a relationship often puts pressure on the other to change – to be more open, more loving, to be different in some way—so there is bound to be times when there is distance in the relationship and when meeting is difficult.

Most likely, one partner is able to tolerate a certain distance more than the other, because maturity, by definition, means our ability to be alone and happy, not focusing on the other person but on ourselves. To say the same thing in another way, the partner with the higher level of consciousness, or the greater degree of spiritual maturity, will find it easier to accept the relationship as it is, because of the ability to be alone, while the other partner will be less able to relax in the moment, less able to be in a state of unconditional love, more busy with thoughts, desires and ambitions.

This is an important understanding for any therapist who deals with the issue of relationship, whether inner or outer, because – as we saw in the previous chapter — it indicates that more can be expected from the side which is more mature and less from the other side. If both sides happen to be on the same plane there is likely to be a certain balance, but whether this will be of joy, dream, or misery is open to question.

To summarize: our inner process of development doesn't follow a straight line, but moves with many twists and turns. Our male side may grow in awareness for some time, without much happening on the feminine side, or vice versa, and then suddenly things may switch around and growth focuses on the opposite polarity. There are bound to be imbalances at different times and we need to respect this rather than wanting things to change too quickly or evenly.

A Shift in Gestalt

One of the problems that frequently arises when working with the inner man-woman polarity is that one side usually has a misunderstanding about his or her essential strength. Sometimes both sides have this misunderstanding. For example, the female side may think that the man is so strong that he can take care of both of them, while she believes herself to be weak and dependent. She may put the man on a pedestal and make herself smaller than she really is. Correspondingly, the male side may believe himself to be stronger and more capable than is really the case.

In a session, the underlying truth of the situation needs to come to light and most probably a therapist will help the more mature side to understand the reality first. As part of this process, the therapist will invite the client to question conventional beliefs about human qualities like strength, love, freedom and responsibility. For example, what is considered strong in society may be only a façade that hides fear; what is believed to be humbleness may prove to be deeply egoistic, while a seemingly self-confident person may actually be quite lost. The truth is that people are easily deceived by appearances and often forget to question the truth of what is presented to them.

Example: 'Weak' Woman, 'Strong' Man

Claudia came for a session, because she felt unsatisfied with her job and her overall level of happiness. When we explored the relationship dynamic between her inner male and female, the man appeared to have an over-inflated sense of self-esteem while the inner female was looking up to him, thinking him to be a great guy and allowing him to make most of the decisions.

Claudia's female side felt incapable of taking any steps or decisions by herself and kept looking for the man's approval. However, during the session, the woman started to be aware that, left by herself, she actually knew very well what things in life she enjoyed doing, like dancing and singing, or being creative with her hands.

The problem was that, in real life, Claudia didn't have much time to pursue any of her likings as she worked long hours in an office for a computer company — work she did mainly for financial reasons. In terms of the inner relationship, although the female admired the man, who provided financial security for her, she also felt deeply unsatisfied, as he did not have much time for her, or express any interest in the things she liked to do (by the way, this accurately reflected her relationship with her boyfriend).

When exploring the male side, we found a character who considered himself to be very important, looking down on the female and seeing her as incapable of making a living by herself. When asked if he liked his present job, he said yes, but it was more the money that he appreciated than the work itself. On further inquiry, it seemed difficult for him to say what he really liked to do; in fact, he felt quite lost and was in considerable tension.

In the session, the female had more presence and therefore more capacity for change. She was asked to take responsibility for her choices, rather than remaining passive and expecting the man to take care of her. When this happened, it was relatively easy for her to take a decision to create space in her life for doing what she really wanted. The challenge for her was to insist on following her choices, even when the man was disapproving.

As soon as she was able to do this, the man became shaky and it became apparent that he needed her and felt lost without her. Underneath his pride, he was actually tired and needed time to rest. In the following work, step by step, the woman took more responsibility and began to explore her choices in life, in relationship, in work and in her daily routine. After initial resistance the man, in proportion to the woman becoming stronger, started to feel relieved of a burden.

This is just one example of a possible dynamic between the inner male and female polarities. The basic work is to help each side find and follow his or her true nature. In one case, it may be simply a question of taking 15 minutes a day to do what one really enjoys; for someone else, it may mean to leaving a job, or starting to write a book, or leaving town and moving to a nicer location. It can be something very practical and specific.

In general, as already indicated, the therapist can expect more from the character who is more connected to truth and who has more presence, and less from the one who is not so mature. This is in tune with the understanding that freedom is an essential quality of love, including freedom to 'take space,' to be unavailable for the other, to be preoccupied… and so on. But this is exactly the opposite of what we do when we pressure the one who is unavailable, judging him, or her, for not giving more love.

Example: Please Give Me More Space
The male side was a social character, but appeared somewhat

depressed and enclosed, trying to take care of the female materially, but being emotionally withdrawn and complaining about not having enough 'space' when it came to making decisions. The female side was confused about the man, but clear about what she wanted. The following is an excerpt from what each character said, using the Gestalt method:

Male: I want to contribute more and have more space to take the initiative.

Female: Last time when I listened to you, when we decided where to go for a holiday, it turned out to be really boring.

Male: I agree, but at least I tried. I agree that it was not the best holiday we had, but I am learning.

Female: You also told me that you enjoy following what I decide.

Male: You are right, but still I feel I should have some more space and more responsibility.

In this dialog we can see that the man behaves like a classic camel, he is collapsed and asks the other's permission rather than making his own choice. The female is in the role of 'you should' and her concern is more with the man than with herself. Initially, both sides did not show much presence, so the therapist decided to test the ability of both sides for more self-connection.

Therapist to the male side: How do you feel when she makes most of the decisions?

Male (looking sad and miserable): I feel useless and worthless. I want to show her that I can be strong and behave like a man.

The man's misery is related to an unfulfilled desire. He has an ideal about how a man should behave, which arises from his social education and conditioning; it doesn't come from the female pressuring him. Because he is so busy trying to live up to this ideal, he has not even begun to look inside to discover what would bring him joy. Instead, he moves between collapse and the effort of trying to prove his worth.

Therapist to the female side: What happens to you when he says he wants more space, and when you see him collapsed like this?
Female: I feel a bit confused. I used to think he is a great guy, but now he appears very boring. If I don't take charge, nothing happens. Also, I have lots of energy and I don't want to compromise on what I want.

The female side had a dream about the man and, when she sees his reality, she starts judging him and feeling disappointed. Her reaction is that of a lion, who typically says "I want to do what I want."

Therapist to female: Do you feel you have to compromise?
Female: Yes, when he asks for space I feel I have to give it and that irritates me. I don't want to give up what I want.
Therapist: Can you give an example when you felt you did that?
Female: He wanted to move to this big flat and we did, so now we have to pay more rent and I have to work hard; I don't have time any more for meditation, which I used to enjoy a lot. Besides, I really loved our old place, it was so cozy.

Now it becomes clear that the woman is trying to please the man, rather than trusting her own sense of what is good for her; this makes her frustrated and then she reacts as a lion. But it is not really the man who is responsible for that, but her own conditioning, according to which a woman has to follow the man. So she switches between the camel and the lion: as a camel, she tries to make the man happy but ends up taking care of him; as a lion, she becomes resentful and tough. For her, the solution is to only take care of herself, not giving up her sense of direction and, when the man decides things, letting him carry the consequences of his choices. This will help her to remain satisfied and will also help the man learn to take responsibility for his decisions.

We see here that both sides are caught in their own conditioning, which makes them lose self-connection. The work now is to help the stronger side follow her sense of direction without dominating the other; in other words, not to give up her own truth for the hope of being loved.

Therapist (to the female side): According to you, how much time would you like per day for meditation and where would you like to live?

Female: I would like two hours for meditation and I don't need such a big flat. I like it more cozy.

Therapist (asking the male side): What do you feel about that?

Male (relieved): Yes, this place really is too expensive, but I wanted to show her that I am a strong guy.

The weaker side, in this case the man, needs to learn to look inside himself, rather than trying to compete with the woman. If the woman takes care to remain satisfied, she will be able to be loving without following the man. This also serves the man and his need for love and appreciation. Then he will be able to relax more, learn to look inside and eventually find something that is fulfilling for him. This, however, may take time and until then, the woman should not expect too much from the man.

The session continued.

Allowing Each Their Freedom

These examples demonstrate that our male and female energies can look like two persons living inside us. Sometimes we act from the male energy and sometimes from the female energy. Our growth is hindered and problems arise when we follow the one that is less connected, rather than listening to the one who has more presence and is more able to find fulfillment alone. If we allow freedom to both, without pressure, and at the same time ask the stronger one to actualize his or her needs, then both sides can start to develop on their own, which will make a meeting possible at some time in the future. However, this meeting will be a spontaneous happening, not a desired goal arising from effort.

Exercise: Meeting the Inner Male and Female

Here is an exercise in which you can begin to become acquainted with your own inner man and inner woman.

Arrange a time and place where you can be relaxed and at ease, without disturbance, for at least 20-30 minutes. You will need a notepad and pen, so have them handy.

Stand comfortably, feet shoulder-width apart, knees slightly bent, with your eyes closed and your weight evenly distributed in both legs.

When you are ready, begin to lean to the right, slowly bringing your body-weight into your right leg. This is not intended to be a 'stress' position, such as we find in bio-energetics, so don't become uncomfortable; keep your left foot on the floor for balance.

Notice how it is for your right leg to carry your body's weight. Is it strong enough to do this? How does it feel? Then extend this awareness up the right side of your body: right side of the pelvis, right side of the torso, right arm and shoulder, right side of the face. Notice how this side of your body feels, sensing it from within.

Imagine that just in front of you there is a blank sheet of paper, or a plain white canvas. Invite a picture of a male figure, to be drawn on the canvas in front of you, using your inner eye, like an invisible painter. If it helps, imagine that there is a paintbrush or crayon in your right hand and, with eyes closed, allow your hand to move across the canvas. Let your intuition do this for you. See the outline of this person appearing.

Notice which parts of the body appear first, or which don't appear at all. What type of body, what kind of face does this man have? Is he tall or small, thin or fat, young or old? What kind of clothes is he wearing? Are they expensive clothes, working clothes, contemporary clothes, or clothes from an earlier time? Watch the picture that is being drawn. Notice the background, the surrounding environment. In what situation is this person? Is he sitting, standing, or moving? Is he alone, or with other people? What do you notice about this person's character? Is he happy or unhappy? Angry or sad? What is this person's attitude towards life? What does he say about life? How does he relate with others? Take a moment to become aware of anything else that may fill in the identity of this character.

When you have finished, slowly let go of the image, or 'painting,' and return to yourself, here and now, in this moment. Open your eyes, go to your notepad and write down the main points, so that you can easily remember the features and qualities of this male character.

When you have finished writing, stand up and move your body: stretch, jump, dance, shaking off the male image and coming back to your normal self.

Stand comfortably, close your eyes, then slowly shift your weight onto your left leg, as you did before with the right leg. Do everything in the same way with the left side of your body, going up from the feet to the head, checking how you feel on this side, noticing any differences from the right side. Perhaps it feels stronger or weaker, more alive or less sensitive, lighter or darker.

Then, invite the picture of a woman to be drawn by an invisible painter, allowing it to emerge in front of your inner eye. Imagine as if you are looking at a screen and a female person starts appearing there. Or, if it helps, imagine that your left hand is moved by a hidden force and is drawing the picture on a canvas in front of you. Take your time.

What do you see in this woman? Is she young or old, thin or fat, short or tall, plain or beautiful? Do you see her whole body or only parts of it? Is she very feminine? What does she wear — simple working clothes, or expensive gowns and dresses? Does she look contemporary, or from another time? In what situation do you see her? In what surrounding is she located? What is in the background? Notice other characteristics of this woman. Is she happy or sad? Is she fearful, suspicious, or trusting? Does she look vulnerable or does she seem hard? What is her attitude toward life? What does she say about life?

When you have absorbed all that you can about this female character, slowly let go of her image and come back to your normal self, in the present, here and now. Make a few notes so that you can easily remember the main features and qualities of this woman.

Then take a deep breath and stretch your body, shaking off the image.

Take a short break, then sit down and review your notes about the man and the woman. Imagine these two people, your inner man and your inner woman, living together. What would this be like? Who would be dominating, taking what decisions? Ask yourself if this reminds you of any relationship that you have experienced in your life.

Now you can review the main points of this chapter again, in the context of these two characters that have been revealed. You can also insert your own inner man and inner woman into the dialogues of the examples; perhaps, in some way, they are relevant to your own situation; perhaps you can see who is taking too much responsibility, or too little, who is taking too much space, or too little, in your life. This will help you begin to understand the dynamics of your inner male-female polarity.

~

Part Two

Working with People

In this section we will describe principles of working with people based on the understanding that has been outlined in the first part of this book. Anyone who works with people needs to understand not only the root of a problem, but also how to respond to a client in a way that supports his process of growth, which is basically a growth in consciousness.

As we have seen, a counselor provides a situation and an atmosphere in which energy can shift from mind to being. As part of this process, the counselor has to confront a person's defenses while at the same time nourishing his essential being, and the way this happens will vary according to the type of client. In this section we will be looking in more depth at different ways to do this.

Our exploration will not be method-oriented, because in the process of helping people one can apply these insights to a wide range of different therapeutic techniques, methods and situations. As should be clear by now, it is not primarily the method that helps people, but how a counselor or helper uses and works with it.

To help us examine general principles as to how personal growth can be supported, I will divide a therapy session, or counseling session, into three phases: Support, Confrontation and Pendulation, Integration.

~

Chapter Nine

Phase One: Giving Support

Most schools of therapy will agree on the importance of building trust between a client and his counselor because unless there is a trusting and loving atmosphere there is little possibility for transformation. In NLP this is called 'rapport,' in Star Sapphire Energy work it is called 'supporting resonance,' pointing to the need for supporting a person's presence and his ability to observe his own process. In trauma work, it is called 'resourcing a person,' which relates to finding events in a person's life that he experiences as supportive and relaxing.

Even though each concept is slightly different, they all point to the central importance of giving the client a feeling of trust, relaxation and "at ease" before any problem or difficulty is examined. It also depends on how much trust a person brings to a session, how disturbed he may be, how identified with a particular issue. In other words, at the very beginning of a session the therapist will have to sense a client's degree of presence and his ability to be relaxed and watchful.

Here, I want to remind the reader of what was said in chapter two, that all problems are related to some kind of identification. For example, the more one is identified with one's body, the more irritation or anxiety one will feel when the body is sick. Conversely, the more one has the capacity to be watchful, the less identified one will be with an issue, so, as you can imagine, some clients will be strongly identified with their issues and less watchful, while others will be less identified and more watchful.

The capacity to be watchful and unidentified grows as a person's meditative consciousness grows.

Support: What it Means

As far as support is concerned, some clients will need a lot of it — for some the whole session will be nothing but a process of finding and giving support — while others who already have this ability will be less in need. One can think of it this way: a person, who already has a certain integrity and strength can be challenged, can be confronted, and will not collapse or feel bad about himself as a result. However, when one does this with a person who is less in contact with his own being, or who is less confident about himself, then this may be damaging and the person will feel bad about himself rather than benefiting from being challenged.

Let us look into what 'support' actually means. From what we have understood so far it is clear that support is more about helping a person to become dis-identified with any problem than trying to help by "problem-solving" in the ordinary way. In other words, it is about helping someone find presence. We gave hints about this in chapter three and more detailed examples will be provided in this chapter.

Commonly, support can be misunderstood as being nice, pleasing, sympathetic or comforting. Sometimes we behave like this in daily life when a friend or colleague is in difficulty and we offer comfort to that person. For example, somebody says, "I feel I am unworthy, nobody likes me..." and in response we give assurances: "No, it's not true, you're a good friend and I like you very much."

However, what we ordinarily mean by 'support' is not what is meant in a therapeutic sense. In therapy, we support by reminding a client about some experience that he made in the past, or some resource, or personal quality which he naturally possesses but has forgotten, or with which he has lost contact.

Gautam Buddha once said that his work is to help people remember who they really are. He called it 'right remembrance,' or 'Samasati.' It is the art of remembering what is true in us, what is our nature. Similarly, in therapy we support a client to come out from a negative tendency of the mind by giving attention to the positive in him. How this can be done practically, in a session? How can the therapist know and find what is positive in a client's psyche? We will soon address this issue, but first there are a few other points to consider.

What is Real?

One of Osho's fundamental insights into the nature of human beings is that the ego is a false entity, something the individual creates, starting in early childhood, in response to upbringing, education and social inter-action with parents, peers and others. Because we are identified with this false personality we believe that it is real, and because it has many qualities that we do not like we start fighting with it. But the struggle proves ultimately futile because essentially we are fighting with something that does not exist. It is like fighting with a shadow.

In order to understand that the ego is just a shadow, we need to have some experience of our true nature, our essential being. Spiritual therapy is an effort to support the being and expose the ego. But before we can benefit from a therapist's attempt to expose the falseness of the ego, we need to have some experience of being; we need to know the difference between mind and being, at least to some degree.

For example, one may have a certain ego-related belief about oneself, such as "I cannot ask for help." Now, the more one believes this to be true, the more one behaves accordingly. It is like blowing up a balloon: the more air you pump into it, the bigger it gets. But this belief may be just an idea, with little reality to it. In fact, it can happen that a client makes this statement to a therapist in a session, thereby already proving it is untrue, at least partially, because even to book a session demonstrates the client's ability to ask for help. So a good intervention may be to remind the client about this fact rather than reinforcing the existence of the 'problem' by trying to analyze his apparent helplessness.

Is It True?

When one sincerely questions one's own beliefs, one may be able to enter into what is real. Byron Katie, an American therapist and spiritual teacher, has developed an effective strategy to question beliefs in a series of steps, and the first and most important step is to ask oneself: "Am I absolutely sure that this particular belief is true?" Often, when confronted with such a question, we cannot really say 'yes.' This can be a first step to shift our perception and awaken an awareness of what is real in us.

When we work on an issue we give energy to it and we make it real. So there are issues that do not need to be worked on, because in the first place they are not true. In cases like this, the issue's existential reality needs to be questioned and the approach is more of seeing and understanding than analyzing.

When a therapist is not clear about which issues deserve attention and which do not, he may find himself entering a long therapy process with a client in which a great deal of analyzing and interpreting occurs, but there is little result in terms of actual change. Of course, the client may not know his real issue — in fact most clients do not know — but the therapist needs to have an awareness of what is real and what is a fantasy, a creation of the mind.

Feeling Touched by Presence

We described how to find a state of presence as a therapist. When he is in this state, a therapist can feel when a client enters a similar space, because the therapist's own sense of presence will be enhanced. The therapist will feel expanded inside, something we may call "being touched." When this happens, a therapist knows that the client acted from presence, or his expression showed a certain truth, and this usually deserves recognition and support. When a therapist does not feel this inner expansion then the client's statement is most probably coming from the mind and giving it too much attention can be draining and fruitless.

However, we need distinguish 'being touched' from other moments when we use the same expression, because saying "I feel touched" may simply show how much we are identified with another person and his issue.

For example, someone talks about his pain and it reminds us of something we experienced ourselves and as a result we may even start to feel a similar pain. This kind of 'being touched' is often experienced, but in therapy it is something to be avoided if one truly wants to help another person. To prevent confusion it would be better to say that we feel the truth of what the other expresses, or we notice his presence. Of course, it can still have the quality of touching the heart, but the therapist will not feel in any way personally involved with what is being expressed.

In moments when a therapist feels this, he knows that his client has spoken or acted from presence. There may also be outer signs for presence, for example when a client takes a deep breath of relaxation, or when he settles more comfortably into the chair, or when he smiles or visibly relaxes in some other way. But these outer signs can also be deceptive and it is ultimately the therapist who has to decide if he can recognize the truth when it is uttered.

Paying Attention to Presence

Moments of relaxation or presence can happen rarely, occasionally, or frequently during a session, depending on the client, and it is something to which a therapist should pay attention. It may be more important than the content of what the client is talking about, as it gives an indication of what is needed in a session. So it is important not to get absorbed only in the act of listening to the topic, or issue, but also to be aware of how the client is relating to what he is talking about. For example, is he tense or relaxed? Does he accept or reject the issue? Is he aware of the real issue, or not? Is he identified with it, or attached to it?

Supporting a person usually means reminding him about those moments when he was able to relax and was present, in a state of 'yes' and acceptance. When such moments happen in daily life we do not usually pay much attention to them, as we tend to be more occupied with negative problems and situations. In a way, this tendency is natural, since we want to get rid of the negative — that's why we focus on it.

It may help to remind ourselves that a negative state is only an absence, without substance of its own, so rather than remaining focused on the negative one should look for the positive, or at least become conscious of the positive as well. If one feels fear, one needs to look for trust, or for what is relaxing. If one is in pain, one needs to search for some moment of joy. The negative cannot be dealt with directly, or exclusively. Both exist, the negative and the positive, but it is a question how and where we direct our attention.

Example: Helping a Client Discover Presence

Support may mean that a therapist reminds the client about those moments in the past when he was not identified with his problem, or it may mean helping the client to discover such moments within the context of the session itself. But it always requires that the therapist himself is relaxed and present.

These extracts from a session, involving a client with little presence, illustrate how this works:

*The client's manner is tense and somewhat 'speedy;' he is talking rapidly
    and is not breathing very deeply.*
Client: I feel so tense and restless. I don't know what to do.
The therapist does not say anything, just waits in a relaxed manner.
After a while, the client slows down slightly and breathes out noticeably.
Therapist: How are you feeling now?
Client: A little better, but still tense.
Therapist: Is there anything that is relaxing for you right now?

Client: It is good to breathe more deeply... and I notice my legs.

Therapist: Take a moment to be aware of your breathing and sense your legs.

For a moment, the client smiles but then turns serious again.

Client: I am too much in the head and I am so worried that I won't be able to solve this problem.

Therapist after a pause: I notice you smiled for a moment when you became aware of your legs. Did you notice that?

Client nods, doesn't say anything.

Therapist: What do you notice right now?

Client: I feel better.

(the session continues)

The therapist rests and waits for a pause in the client's monologue before asking a question. He also chooses to give attention to small moments of relaxation rather than entering the problem, or asking the client to change.

Later in the same session:

Client: I am trying to recover the relaxation from before, but I cannot.

Therapist: Yes, trying to relax makes one really tense.

Client laughs.

Therapist: Or trying not to repress or not to be in the mind....it is quite a struggle.

Client: It is true.

Therapist: If you are not trying anything right now. How are you?

Client: Exhausted. I want to relax.

Therapist: How is it to feel exhausted?

Client: Not so good. I have no energy.

Therapist: If you have the idea that you should always be full of energy, then you are creating an impossible situation for yourself. Sometimes I enjoy allowing myself to totally collapse; it is a deep let go.

Client lightens up: I never looked at it this way.

Desire and effort creates tension, even the desire to relax. A feeling of exhaustion indicates how much effort one has been making. The therapist acknowledges the client's present state without trying to help or change him. Obviously, the client was attached to the idea that to be energetic is better than to have no energy, and the therapist has now challenged that belief.

Highlighting Self-Awareness

Client: I feel I am not good enough, if I don't do anything.

Therapist: Yes, that is called conditioning. Can you just check how your body is right now?

Client (without really tuning into his body): Not good. I have no energy to do anything right now.

Therapist: And that bothers you?

Client: Yes.

Therapist: So you want to feel full of energy all the time. You are asking a lot. Usually, there is a natural rhythm: one moment high energy, one moment low energy... what difference does it make? But you expect a lot from yourself, impossible things.

Client, laughing: Yeah, that is true.

Therapist: Is there any part in you that can enjoy this moment of just being?

Client: My arms are happy to just not do anything. But I also really feel this urge to get rid of the tension in my solar plexus.

The client quickly picks up his effort again.

Therapist: Let's come back to this later and just take a moment to stay with feeling your arms. I also noticed you were just laughing a moment ago. How was that?

Client.: I noticed that I am not accepting, not surrendering.

Therapist: That sounds like a good insight; you became aware of your wanting. But I noticed that in the moment when you were smiling just now you didn't want anything. You were just smiling, did you notice that? I think that's great. You started laughing about yourself.

I feel that's wonderful. Most people can't do that. They remain serious about themselves. And you just had a wonderful moment of being non-serious about yourself. Can you see that? How is it, when you see that?

Client: Very relaxing.

Obviously, in this part of the session, the therapist does not enter any issue with the client, but only works on finding and supporting presence.

It is important that the therapist does not want his client to relax, otherwise he would be putting pressure on him in a subtle way. He simply works on the client's awareness. Also one can see how he gives support to a brief moment of self-awareness and non-seriousness. He highlights it.

As a result, the client's state of relaxation is slowly growing during the session, without being asked to relax. Out of habit, he may go back into effort and desire, then the therapist will continue in the same style and the client's relaxation may go deeper still. In this part of a session, the content of the client's desire or problem does not really matter much; his awareness of the moment, without any future goal, is the solution.

The principle employed here is that when the client goes into desire, the therapist relaxes and allows it to happen without trying to take the client out. When the client does come out, which is bound to happen sooner or later, then that moment receives support from the therapist. There is no goal in the session. If one has a goal, one is immediately in a state of tension to reach it.

Appreciating Small Steps

In the rest of the session, the therapist helps the client begin to appreciate small steps of awareness and to give up the habit of high expectations. As the client's awareness and presence grows, issues can start to be explored. Awareness and relaxation cannot be created through desiring them, or making them a goal; rather, they come to us when we are receptive and undemanding.

It is important that the therapist distinguishes which actions of a client arise from saying 'yes' to himself and which come from effort, or trying. Both actions may look alike, but they are totally different. Support, in this context, means that the therapist supports those moments when the client says 'yes' to himself and makes a point of magnifying or highlighting such moments so that the client becomes aware of them.

This ability to recognize moments of 'yes' is the basis of effective therapy and the key to spontaneous growth, and requires the counselor to be in touch with his own sense of inner presence.

Chapter Ten

Phase 2: Confrontation and Pendulation

Support is not the only thing a therapist can do in a session. He may also confront the client, but as we mentioned earlier, if the client lacks presence then this is likely to create tension and will not be beneficial. If, however, the client has enough presence, confrontation will lead to a deepening of his connection with his essential nature, because through this process he will become more free from identification with his personality and mind structure.

The need for support, the readiness for confrontation or challenge, can be understood when we compare it to the functioning of the human body's nervous system: a healthy nervous system that has not been exposed to overwhelming levels of traumatic stress in the past has a resiliency that enables it to handle difficulties well, without the need of being supported. On the other hand, a nervous system that has been subjected to traumatic stress beyond its capacity for self-regulation will be less able to adjust to even small degrees of stress and tension; rather, it will be more in need of stabilizing support. In the latter case, exposure to challenge by a therapist needs to happen in a slow and gentle way.

From a psychological perspective, a person who has a higher level of maturity or self-awareness will probably be less identified when examining his own personality or mind structure. It will be easier for such a person to stay in touch with his witnessing consciousness during confrontation. On the other hand, a person who has little or no experience of meditation will get identified more easily and may feel bad about himself, or start to defend, project, rationalize or resort to any of the defense mechanisms that traditional psychoanalysis has described so extensively.

Just as it is necessary for a counselor, who works with an issue of trauma, to find out how much resiliency is contained in a client's nervous system, in a similar way it is helpful to understand a person's level of consciousness and potential for self-awareness. Then the therapist can determine in each session how much or how little support is necessary and how deeply and directly an issue can be worked on.

What Does 'Confrontation' Mean?

Confrontation does not mean 'attack;' it simply means to face, or focus on, a personality issue. For example, a client has a problem dealing with money and the therapist helps him to look for the root of the problem. In the support phase, the therapist by-passed the issue that was creating tension for the client, but now he invites the client to look into it. This can happen gently, or in a more sharp way, but the purpose is always the same: to bring a client's awareness to the way his desires keep him separate from life. In other words, separate from what is he rejecting or avoiding in himself.

In speaking of man's longing for more expanded states of consciousness, many mystics have pointed out that it is our desires that prevent the natural flow of the life force within us. The combination of all our desires creates our character, personality, or ego, and it is this fixed structure that does not allow us to respond to new situations in a spontaneous way, but instead forces us into a predetermined and confining pattern. We have seen examples of this when examining the camel and lion patterns of relating.

In the phase of 'support' a counselor searches for manifestations of a person's being, or presence, while in the phase of 'confrontation' he addresses that which hinders the being. We can compare it to someone who falls asleep or is lost in daydreams. In 'support' we search, or wait, for moments when he is close to being awake, while in confrontation we take hold of the person's shoulder and shake him. Of course, trying to awaken someone who is deeply asleep may be difficult, or shocking, or may be met with strong resistance. To do the same thing to someone who is only half asleep may require just a gentle touch, and it may be received very differently. In other words, a counselor will need to know what is likely to be most beneficial for the client and what approach is going to be received better.

Some people compare the work of a therapist to that of a gardener. When a plant is small or has just sprouted it needs support, protection and nourishment in order to grow. Pruning leaves and branches at this stage may damage or even kill it. However, once a plant has grown into a tree there comes a moment when pruning by a skilled gardener can be tremendously helpful in making the tree stronger and more integrated. This is the stage of confrontation and many times it is painful, but no strength can develop without it. At this stage, a therapist who continues to give only support will simply create weakness.

What is 'Pendulation'?

The term 'pendulation' comes from the vocabulary of Somatic Experiencing, an advanced method of trauma resolution. In trauma work, pendulation describes the process of repeatedly going in and coming out of traumatic material. First, the therapist resources a person — what we call support — then he invites the client to enter into the issue that has caused the trauma, starting gently from the periphery. When the client gets too activated, too upset or stressed, the therapist helps the client to again focus on his resources so that he can calm down. This process of swinging back and forth between the traumatic event and personal resources is called 'pendulation'. With each swing of the pendulum one slowly enters the trauma more deeply, balancing this with going deeper into the resources.

The purpose of pendulation is to avoid immediate, head-on

confrontation with a traumatic event, since direct confrontation may actually reinforce the psychological wound rather than helping it to heal.

In a general way, we can say that it is possible to use pendulation as a basic principle in almost every therapy session. First, a therapist makes sure a client is grounded, feels trust and support, and has a certain degree of relaxation. Only then will the therapist confront the issue that the client presents, knowing as he does so that this may cause a certain amount of distress and discomfort to the client. When this gets too much, or the client gets overwhelmed, or too identified with the issue, the therapist will again return to some topic that helps the client feel more at ease. In this way, the session continues and one can compare it to the swing of a pendulum: with each swing the client enters more deeply into the issue and deeper into relaxation.

There is another way to describe this process: we mentioned earlier in the book that mind and being are two different aspects that we address in a session. Support means that the therapist focuses on presence and reminds a client about his being without paying much attention to his desires. When a client is rooted in his being, the therapist switches the focus to the mind and enters into personality issues, helping a client first to express his desires and then to come out of desire and relax into what is.

When a client loses his ability to watch personality issues and gets too identified with his desires, beliefs or judgments, the therapist switches the focus away from the mind and back towards the being, again working on presence. In this way, he moves back and forth between mind and being, gradually bringing more light and awareness to aspects of the client's personality that have roots in the deeper layers of the mind.

Being is a positive force, while the mind's tendency is negative. As we mentioned earlier, the negative is really just an absence of the positive, so rather than trying to resolve negative qualities like anger or fear we need to look for positive qualities, like love and trust, making their presence felt more clearly in the client's psyche. A client's tendency to focus on the absence of something has to be balanced by helping him to realize in what way the positive also exists in him.

Pendulation is really about balance. When a person feels too involved in the negative and in what is missing, we remind him about the positive that also exists in him. When a person feels too satisfied with himself, we remind him about issues that also need to be addressed.

Rejection and Acceptance

The issue that a client brings to the session is not as important as how he relates to it: how much awareness he has about it, how strongly he is identified with it, and so on. In other words, the context of the facts is more important than the facts themselves. For example: a person enters a room angrily but denies that he is angry; while another person enters in a similar state but is aware of his own anger, perhaps even accepting that this is the case.

Both facts are the same, but the two individuals relate to them in very different ways. If both come to counseling sessions for personal work, the counselor will need to deal with them differently. In the first case, after an initial period of establishing trust and making the client aware of 'positive' sides of himself, the therapist may help him become aware of his anger and accept it. In the second case, he may directly begin to examine the roots and reasons for the 'problem' and what is hidden underneath.

In general, the more a client is identified with a 'problem,' the less chance is there to examine it. First, a client needs to establish some kind of distance, or watchfulness, then he can look at an issue. The more a client desires to fix or change anything, the less possibility for transformation. What we want to get rid of will persist, because, as we have already seen, desire is a denial of what is, and only by accepting what is do we give ourselves the key to inner transformation.

When we work with a client to create presence, a certain distance to his issue is created. Once distance is achieved, the client can start observing the issue until distance is again lost; then again the therapist will need to help the client become rooted in being present. This is the process behind the need to pendulate.

Coming Out of Identification

The process of finding distance and coming out of identification is really what meditation is about. To be in a state of meditation is to be free from identification with the personality, including our emotions and our thinking process. However, meditation is not an easy art to master in the sense that, while we may be able to sit silently with eyes closed for a period of time, a certain depth is often missing that keeps the experience superficial. There are too many layers of suppressed desires and denied emotions that do not allow us to penetrate and witness deeper aspects of our personality.

Counseling and therapy can provide a bridge, helping people to experience deeper layers of the mind in an atmosphere of love and acceptance. A therapist can provide a loving atmosphere and his acceptance of the client will make it easier for the client to love himself; this, in turn, will make it easier for a client to observe and become aware of previously suppressed parts of his psyche.

True watchfulness is possible only in a loving atmosphere, otherwise one cannot allow oneself to see that which one has been rejecting for most of one's life. Maybe this is the reason why Gautam Buddha, in his famous Diamond Sutra, instructed his disciples: love yourselves first, then watch. Self-love comes before watchfulness.

To recap: as we said earlier, each client has a different potential to be watchful. Some clients are identified with their problems and so there is little possibility to examine issues. First, these clients will need to be supported and only then can an issue be examined, but even during examination the therapist's emphasis may suddenly need to change: the client may again become identified and then the therapist goes back to support. If too many issues or 'defects' are pointed out by a therapist during a single session, then a client may lose the awareness that 'this is not me' and may start to feel bad about himself. Immediately, the therapist needs to move back to supporting the positive until the person has brightened up again and can be watchful.

So a therapist has to observe each client and become aware of signs of identification and discomfort. How much discomfort a person can tolerate without being overwhelmed depends on various things, including the degree of awareness or consciousness exhibited by a client.

Stages of Transformation

A person with little experience of meditation is, by definition, full of desires and will be more insistent to get these desires fulfilled, because his sense of self, or 'I,' is strongly identified with realizing them. For example, he may want to be successful in business, he may want to gain public recognition, he may want to excel in sport... his sense of 'who I am' is closely related to his ambitions. So, in a session, the first thing a therapist will need to do is introduce some understanding of the difference between the social mask of personality, which is created by our conditioning, and the unique individuality with which we are born.

However, a session is not just a process of showing a client the hidden aspects of his personality. It has more to do with tuning into a person's capacity to understand a particular issue at this stage in his personal development in consciousness. Change does not happen because we want it to happen, but because something inside us is ready for a shift, which is often beyond anybody's will. In other words, it is not just a matter of conscious choice, but a response to some kind of maturity manifesting from within. It is something that emerges when we create the right atmosphere for it to happen. Transformation happens through acceptance. It cannot be brought about through effort or will-power, because wanting to be accepting, or wanting to be more conscious, is just another layer of desire.

In this context, pendulation is a process of swinging between something that a person already accepts about himself and something that is still unconscious or rejected. If the degree of acceptance is slight, there will be little possibility to look further into the area of desire. If acceptance is strongly developed, the roots of desire can be explored. This is a simple principle that good therapists apply more or less intuitively, even if they work with different techniques of counseling.

In the following example, taken from a counseling session, it is possible to see what is support and what is confrontation, and how the therapist pendulates between the two. The client is supported to stay in the present and yet challenged to explore what is behind his state of desire.

Support Phase

Client (male): I fell in love with a woman and I want a relationship with her, but she doesn't want to commit herself to me.

Therapist: How do you feel about that?

Client: I feel confused and tense.

Therapist: Take a moment to feel what is happening in your body right now. What do you notice?

Client: My heart is beating strongly and my breathing is uneven, restless.

Therapist: Yes, it can be quite disturbing to be in a situation like that. Give yourself a moment to feel the beating of your heart and your breath. Give them space and time. And then let yourself notice what else is happening in your life right now."

Client (after a while): Now, my heart is becoming a little calmer... my breathing as well. My life is actually quite good at this moment, I have a new house that I like and my work is also going well.

The client is being acknowledged in his situation and supported to be present by connecting to his body. His attention is shifted away from seeing only 'the problem' and his desire. As a result the pressure and tension begins to decrease.

Client: I feel like I want to hold on to something, or run away from something.

Therapist: Where do you feel this energy?

Client: In my arms and legs. It feels like my body wants to move.

Therapist: Can you give your body a little space for that without judging it, or trying to decide what it is?

Up to now, the client has been holding himself still. Now he allows some movement through his arms and legs. He has been under a considerable amount of pressure and now releases some of the tension. He smiles.

As the client relaxes, he also comes more in contact with the repressed energy behind his desire and, as he allows some of this energy to move, he experiences relief. The therapist takes care not to enter the dimension of desire; instead, he focuses on the positive and the relaxation that is happening now.

Therapist: I notice you are smiling and more life is coming into your facial expressions.

Client nods.

The client is mirrored and supported.

Client (picking up what happened before and entering another desire): I sometimes feel that I want to get out of this anxiety. I don't like it.

Therapist: Okay, let's slow things down a little; let's just stay with what is happening right now. Is it anxiety or excitement?

The therapist does not follow the client into the desire, but helps him to stay present by re-framing his experience.

Client (relaxing, laughing and moving the body): Now it is excitement.
Therapist: Okay, let's stay with this for a moment; let's see if you can enjoy this much excitement right now and explore what your body wants to do with it.
Client: It looks like a new possibility, it's great.

Rather than only enjoying the moment and his body, the client starts again to think about the future. Now his feeling of excitement is related to a dream about the future. Anxiety indicates fear of not getting what one desires; excitement indicates the hope of getting it.

Here we see how important it is for a therapist to notice the subtle difference between when enjoyment relates to relaxing into the present moment and when it arises from dreaming about the future. Just a moment before, the client's enjoyment was related to the present, now it has moved into the future.

However, at this stage the therapist does not confront the client with his hopes; rather, he helps the client become more connected to the present through awareness of his body.

Therapist: Allow your body to explore this feeling of relaxation and aliveness. I see some movements are happening in your face, in your mouth, your hands, color comes to your face… a smile happens.
Client: When I put my attention on the feeling of expansion, I feel more wide, more present. I feel more trust in myself.

Confrontation Phase

Some time later:
Therapist: Let's talk about the reason why you wanted this session. You said that your girlfriend doesn't want to commit to a relationship with you, and you feel uncomfortable about that. Obviously, you

don't have the power to change her.

After having been supported, the client is now confronted with the possibility of not getting what he desires.

Client: Yes.

Therapist: Can you let yourself feel what you want from her? And feel the source of this desire in you?

Client: I want her to give me her total 'yes' (he expresses this desire with a strong movement of the hands, as if holding a big object, looking excited).

Through wanting something from the outside, the client is still not looking at what he is avoiding in himself.

Therapist: And how do you feel right now, as she has not given you her total 'yes'?

Client (a bit confused): I feel shaky and insecure.

Therapist: And how is it for you to feel that? How is your body, your legs and arms?

Client (becoming uncomfortable): I am keeping them still (the legs and feet).

The client now goes back into control. He is not ready, or able, at this point to explore the feeling of insecurity, which may touch an old wound of having been manipulated when exposing his vulnerability. The client is now getting too identified with the issue.

So the therapist has to back off and go back to support. Just changing the subject can help already.

Support Phase

Therapist: Let's talk about something else. Let's leave the issue with your girlfriend for the moment. How do you feel being here in this group? (in this case the client was a participant in a workshop).

Client: Quite good.

Therapist: Let yourself notice the other people. No girlfriend is here and nobody wants anything from you. How does that feel?

Client (relaxing and smiling again): I feel happy to be here and I think it is good for me.

Therapist: What exactly do you feel is good for you? What do you enjoy?

Client (looking at people and appearing vulnerable): To be connected with other people and not so concentrated on my own problems.

Therapist: Yes, can you feel your heart right now?

Client nods.

Therapist: So it relaxes you to have contact with others and be in a loving atmosphere, where you do not need to worry and where there are no expectations. Great. Give yourself a moment to feel this.

The therapist again encourages the space of relaxation, acknowledging and mirroring back to the client his vulnerability and what he just realized himself.

Integration Phase

Therapist: It seems you are quite used to situations where something is expected from you, or you expect something from yourself or others. Is this true?

Client: Yes.

Again the therapist swings back to the issue, taking into account that the client's expectation towards his girlfriend is a pressure he also puts on himself; in fact, her reaction is a projection of his own reaction in such situations.

Therapist (without exploring the issue further): So it seems when there is expectation on you from others, or maybe from yourself, you get easily tense and forget yourself.

Client: That's right.

Therapist: But in this moment there is also a certain vulnerability present in you. So you may get tense when you look at another person – what she may do, or not do — but you can also choose to enjoy this feeling of openness in your heart right now. Can you feel that?

Client: Yes, I can... it feels quite new.

Therapist: And that is something that does not depend on anyone else. Can I leave you with this feeling, for the moment, even though we haven't really solved your problem with your girlfriend?

Client: Yes. It seems less important now.

Therapist: For me, this is a positive outcome from the session: that you are more in contact with yourself, enjoying your own space right now, rather than hoping to get something in the future. This is great. We all need to learn this."

Here, the therapist is giving encouragement to a small step the client has made, supporting the positive, while at the same time not giving too much importance to the negative. This session is about learning meditation and relaxation, because the client's ability to be present is not strong enough to make an in-depth exploration of the relationship issue.

On a deeper level, it is apparent that this client wants his girlfriend's commitment in order not to feel his own vulnerability, his own insecurity. The strong desire covers up a rejected part of himself: his own neediness. In general, this is a common situation in love relationships: we want certainty from a partner, because we can't tolerate insecurity. By learning to stay more in the present, we can start to enjoy the vulnerability and aliveness that comes with insecurity, and in this way the future becomes less important.

Creating a Relaxed Atmosphere

From the perspective of inner male-female dynamics, the therapist supported the client's feminine side to stay vulnerable and open, rather than reacting to expectation and pressure. It seems the male side is putting pressure and trying to stay in control in order to avoid insecurity.

In terms of pendulation, we see how the therapist swings between supporting the client and addressing the issue. When the client becomes tense and too identified with his desire, the therapist moves back to support.

It is important to note that the therapist does not pressure his client to become more aware, or ask him to be more vulnerable and less controlling. Rather, he simply changes the subject and waits until the client begins to relax, at which time the client's vulnerability surfaces naturally. Relaxation is a natural state that can happen in an atmosphere of 'not wanting' and the therapist creates this atmosphere by being in a relaxed space himself. When the client relaxes, even if it is only for a brief moment, the therapist points it out to him.

In this session, the solution was not to solve the problem with the girlfriend, but to help the client feel more relaxed about not receiving the certainty he asked for, and to help him understand that this is supportive to his personal growth.

Chapter Eleven

Phase Three: Integration

Integration refers to two processes. First, integration is something that happens at specific moments during a session, when new insights are being absorbed and understood by the client. There is a certain rhythm in a session between looking at an issue and then allowing time for a new understanding to be integrated and absorbed. Second, integration refers to that period towards the end of a session when no new insights are being processed but when the whole work is becoming stabilized and solidified. This usually happens after a process of confrontation and pendulation has been completed and the time required for integration depends on the client and the intensity of the session.

Stages of a Session

The process of a session can be compared to a good novel: it starts slowly, builds steadily in depth and intensity and comes to a peak in the last third of the session, leaving sufficient time at the end for integration and relaxation. This is the general outline.

If a session reaches the client's most important issue too quickly it can create a problem, because there may not have been enough time beforehand to build the support needed to deal with it fully or work through it. Moreover, the remaining part of the session may be too long and the effect of an important insight may be lost or diminished by subsequent developments. In this way, the energy of the session may become flat and the client may leave with a feeling of dissatisfaction. On the other hand, if the peak of the session is reached too late, there will not be enough time for integration and the client may leave in an agitated state without being ready to face the world outside the session room.

Leading a session is like conducting a symphony: it needs to have a certain rhythm, pace and time-frame. This provides a solid basis to the work and also gives a sense of security and clarity to the client. A session is a contract lasting for a specified period and both parties need to be aware of it. If a client starts bringing up an important issue during the closing minutes of a session, as a general rule a therapist should not deal with it but rather make another appointment, or help the client understand that this may be a strategy to avoid dealing with the issue in depth.

At the end of a session, a client should not be in a state of excitement and euphoria, nor in a state of shock, anger or sadness at what has been revealed, but in a more neutral and grounded state that is somewhere in the middle of these extreme emotions. Of course, some degree of emotion or feeling is natural and must be expected, but a state of strong emotion – either positive or negative – is likely to be followed by a swing in the opposite direction. As we know from the process of pendulation, there exists a balancing force, swinging from one polarity to the other, so there is a strong possibility that the more ecstatic one feels then the more deeply agony is likely to arise at another moment, and vice versa.

In other words, energy tends to seek balance and the more one moves to one extreme the more likely it is that the other extreme will manifest, and this can be difficult to bear. There are cases on record of people emerging from deep therapeutic processes in a very "high" state of apparent enlightenment and clarity, who then became extremely confused and disturbed when the downside eventually manifested. Knowing that energy moves like a pendulum, a therapist can help the client to end a session in an ordinary state, grounded in the present moment, in which life appears to be not too fantastic and also not so terrible.

A counselor takes care that the client can reach this state by supporting him, reminding him about the positive elements if he had a shocking realization, or, on the other hand, balancing any 'great' or 'ecstatic' experience by making him aware that his negative tendency is likely to return to some degree, even if he feels relieved from it right now.

This Too Will Pass

There is an ancient teaching story, probably from Sufi origins, that illustrates the value of staying grounded in reality without being swayed too much by extreme states of ecstasy or misery.

A king called his advisors to a meeting one day and asked them to produce something for him that would help him be happy even when he was very miserable, and help him feel sadness even when he was ecstatically happy. For a long time none of his advisors could find any way to do this, but eventually a wise old courtier came to the king and presented him with a golden ring.

"There is a message inside the ring," explained the old man. "But you must not take it out and read it until you are in a state of either extreme despair or extreme happiness."

The king agreed, put the ring on his finger and soon forgot all about its message.

Years passed, then tensions developed with a neighboring country which eventually led to a state of war between the two kingdoms. There was a battle, the king's army lost and he was forced to flee into the mountains, with his enemy in hot pursuit, intent on killing him.

He was riding through a narrow pass when his horse lost a shoe and he was forced to dismount and hide behind a rock. Certain that he would be discovered and killed, he fell into a mood of deep despair, but then suddenly remembered the ring on his finger. He took it off, pulled out the tiny piece of paper from inside it, and read these words:

"This too will pass."

His pursuers galloped by the rock, not seeing the king, and he managed to escape. Gradually, over the next few weeks and months, he was able to gather his troops and wage a campaign against the invaders, and eventually succeeded in getting back his kingdom.

The whole country was celebrating and the palace was full of music, laughter and rejoicing. In the middle of it all, the king glanced down at the ring on his finger, remembered its message, and smiled in understanding.

Keeping Input Appropriate

There should not be much explanation at the end of a session, as this is likely to be intellectual and will bring the client into a thinking mode rather than helping him stay in touch with his feelings and with his new experience of himself. Real understanding goes deeper than intellect, so even if sometimes our mind is not able to grasp a particular realization or concept it may well be accepted and integrated by our being or heart.

This is why a therapist needs to be aware not to give more input than is appropriate or can be digested by the client. One has to remember the mind's tendency to always want more, to always want to explain and rationalize everything, and this can easily happen at the end of a session when the client is getting ready to leave and the ordinary state of thinking resurfaces. A therapist should be aware of this tendency and also make his client conscious of it.

A woman in a session discovered that her attachment to her partner covered up her deep-rooted fear of being left alone, which had its roots in her childhood experience of being abandoned by her mother. In the session, she understood and healed some of her attachment issues and also discovered how she could support herself in daily life without clinging to her partner. When, at the end of the session, she again asked what to do about her relationship and the therapist didn't answer, she got the point and laughed about herself.

In most cases it will be helpful to leave a client to himself, once a session has ended, and not to switch to social and personal relating such as, for example, going together for tea or lunch. Even though this seems self-evident, many therapists are not clear about the dividing line between inter-action with a client in a session and personal contact afterwards. More will be said about this in the next chapter.

Connecting the Beginning with the End

A client usually comes to a session with a particular issue or a question about his life. Often, clients have several questions, problems, or issues and at first may not see how they are connected with each other, or which ones are more significant. During a session, the therapist may sense a need to move away from the client's original question, or specified issue, and deal with another issue that seems unrelated but is in fact more important. Sometimes, the connection to the client's original question becomes clear as a session progresses, but not always. In this case, at the end of the session, the therapist needs to draw a connecting line to the beginning, linking what has transpired with the client's original question. This will make the session complete and the client will feel that his issue has been acknowledged and addressed.

A client came with the issue that his relationship was not working and as a result he was feeling a lot of tension and dissatisfaction. In the session, the real problem became clear: the client had not been exploring his creativity potential and had kept himself in a job that he didn't enjoy for the sake of financial security. The therapist's approach in the session was to support the client's creative talents and encourage him to use them, so there was little or no work on the client's original question. At the end, the therapist explained how this was related to the client's issue about relationship, showing how job dissatisfaction in the workplace was generating a complaining and tense state that created conflict in the relationship as well.

When making such connections, the opposite possibility must also
be borne in mind: attachment to a relationship partner and fear of
losing the other may cause the client to compromise too much,
staying in an unsatisfying job in order to provide financial support
for his partner as well as himself. Then a question about not being
happy at work may find its origin in having a wrong or compro-
mising attitude towards the partner.

Staying Practical, Making Things Clear

Some counselors make the mistake of leaving things vague,
without connecting their work with a client to something real and
practical. We tend to do this in ordinary life as well. For example
we may say to someone, "I have no space for you," which leaves
things unclear. Does it mean I want to end the relationship, or that
I need one day for myself, or simply that I don't want to be
disturbed for the next 30 minutes? Similarly, when I express my
need for love in a relationship, does this mean I want us to be
together all the time, or that I need a hug right now, or that I desire
a more intimate and honest sharing?

In the same way, a counselor should help his client be practical
and direct, rather than vague and general. For example, if the
outcome of a session indicates that it will be helpful for the client
to meditate more, the details should be worked out. What does
'more' mean? One hour a day, once a week on Sunday mornings
for 90 minutes, or ten minutes every night before going to sleep?
Vague intentions do not lead to change; what counts is action in
daily life.

It may also be helpful for a client to be made aware how much
support he has in daily life to make a certain change, or how to
create such support, maybe through changing his place of living,
or by connecting more with certain people, or taking time off
work to spend in a way that is more nourishing to his being.

Staying Out of the Client's Life

Counselors can also make the mistake of being too specific, narrowing things down too much, as if what was revealed in a session now requires a rigid and predetermined procedure to be followed in daily life. This puts pressure and expectations on the client that he should do things in a precise order as part of his next step on the ladder of personal growth.

But what a client does after the session should not be a therapist's concern. What is revealed in a session certainly has meaning, as it will shift something in the client's consciousness, but certain details may be true only for the moment. Moreover, any number of different options may arise from a certain understanding, not of all of which can be covered or anticipated in a session.

Understanding may lead to a certain action in life, or it may not, but this is not the responsibility of the therapist. What a client does after a session has ended should be left to him and a therapist should not even ask the client if he acted upon an insight gained during a session.

Advice is Cheap Therapy

If a particular experience or insight during a session has a strong impact on a client, he may ask the therapist to say more about it at the end, or advise how to integrate it into his life. In addition to what has already been said about the danger of over-explaining things, it is good for a therapist to remember that counseling does not mean to give advice, but to create a situation where a client can make a direct experience.

In fact, case histories in a wide variety of therapeutic disciplines show that many clients make a point of not following a therapist's advice, as a way of maintaining their self-dignity and sense of self-determination, keeping their lives in their own hands. Therefore, one needs to be extremely cautious when a client asks for advice.

As mentioned earlier, it may be helpful for a client to under-stand something on a mental level, but one should remember that the real benefit of a session is not intellectual comprehension, as this has no lasting impact. The effect needs to be on a deeper level than the intellect if it is to have real significance in a client's life. Since the days of Sigmund Freud, psychotherapists have been aware that the unconscious mind is ten times more powerful than the conscious mind and decides most of our actions, so feeding information into the conscious part has limited value.

Further, too much talking and explaining at the end of a session may reduce the actual effect of an experience or inter-vention. It can put the client in the position of a child, who does not understand, and the therapist in the position of an 'expert' or teacher.

A therapist also has to be careful not to try and protect a client from the full effect of a truth that has been revealed. Clients have more strength than the therapist imagines and they know on a deep level what is true. For a therapist not to respect this quality in a client is the psychological equivalent of a medical doctor who decides not to tell a cancer patient that he has only a few months to live. For most clients, facing reality works best. On the other hand, some clients may overestimate their own capacities to heal themselves or to implement change in their lives, and a therapist who can see this tendency should support qualities like patience and the art of making small steps in a new direction.

After Effects

Integration needs time and this understanding should be conveyed during the final stage of a session. A client needs to know that the effects of a session can last for many weeks or months; that a session is not the end, but the beginning of a continuous process, as if one changes tracks on an ongoing journey. How this change can become manifest and be supported in a client's daily life should be examined at the end of a session, especially if the therapist is not working with this client over a long period. Sometimes, it can be of help to identify exercises, or practices, that a client can do by himself.

To say the same thing in a slightly different way, integration means that whatever insights or new understandings have emerged during a session now need time and space to be absorbed by the body and mind until they become part of the client's life. For example, if a client has been confronted with an old belief about himself and has seen that it is no longer accurate, he may still tend to fall back into the old pattern out of habit. In such cases, the therapist may help the client to identify small clues and reminders that can be used in daily life to stay aware of the change.

It is important to connect insights gained in a session to one's daily life — in areas like work, creativity, relationships — and find out what the next practical step might be, rather than having ideas and expectations beyond the client's actual possibility.

For many years, a client has been working in a factory job that no longer matches her creative potential, but she is afraid that if she quits without knowing what comes next she will soon be without money. In the session, it was found that she has a good potential for working with people and has already been partially trained in this field, but has never really explored these skills. The work in the session was to help the client find out what will be her next step towards her aspiration in working with people. She saw that she did not need to give up her factory job, but could safely reduce her working hours to the point where she had space and time to explore her potential while still earning enough money to pay her bills.

Time: A Primary Resource

We sometimes forget that time is one of our primary resources. An insight about oneself may be come in a sudden, unexpected and powerful way, but it usually takes time to consolidate this insight and allow it to affect different aspects of our daily lives. Growth can happen slowly, sometimes so slowly that we may not think we are moving at all, and yet when we look back over the span of a year we may be able to see a significant difference in our behavior and our way of dealing with personal issues.

Many clients are in a hurry to change and want to be 'fixed.' While acknowledging their suffering, it is important to help them understand that real change happens more as a by-product of greater self-understanding than as a result of a deliberate effort; it is the by-product of awareness and acceptance, and all session work should be focused on supporting these two fundamental qualities.

When the pressure to change disappears, transformation becomes possible. This basic view of inner transformation needs to be brought to the attention of the client so he can see how it applies to the issue he has brought to the session.

A man came to a session with the issue of wanting to be stronger and more self-confident in his work in order to reach a higher position in his company. During the session, it became clear that he had a deep, underlying need for love, especially for his father's recognition and approval, and his desire to be stronger in his profession came from a denial of this need. The work in the session focused on the client learning to enjoy vulnerability and understanding that true strength is connected to love, which was a very new concept for him, and clearly a different priority from wanting to succeed in the competitive world of business while inwardly remaining a beggar. It was about recognizing that the process of growing in love takes its time and that an ambitious attitude will not support this. He learned to tolerate moments of frustration, when left with an unfulfilled desire, rather than wanting to cover up his deeper needs through corporate success.

In this chapter, we have looked at general considerations related to counseling, which means that specific details in each case will vary and will need to be worked out in each session. Much also depends on the level of a client's maturity. The more mature the client, the less need for the therapist to support or help the integration process; the less mature the client, the more need for the therapist to take care that the process is not rushed and that the foundation is stable.

Ultimately, therapy should lead to a state where insights are integrated into the client's body and mind through his own self-regulation without any need for active help from the side of the therapist. Nor does the client need to remember exactly what happened in a session. To use an analogy with allopathy, once the medicine has been taken, there is no need to remember what was said on the label and how many spoonfuls were required. One allows it to have its own effect in its own time.

Chapter Twelve

The Attitude of the Therapist

In my book on Family Constellation I talk about the attitude required of a practitioner in a specialized therapeutic field, but the same qualities can be applied to therapists working with people in general. In particular, I describe how a combination of presence, relaxation and warm-heartedness in the therapist can create a state of 'cool love' that means he does not want anything from the client and he is free of preconceived ideas or plans about what is supposed to happen during a session.

In the beginning of this book, I mention how the quality of presence helps us to get out of the grip of identification with the mind, which is an essential step in moving away from a 'problem' orientation towards a deeper state of being. It is the therapist's presence that serves as a catalytic agent to facilitate this process of dis-identification in the client. In a session, his vibe is infectious; just as being in the company of a sick person may make one begin to feel sick, so being in the company of a person in a state of presence will also encourage presence in the other.

But this is not the only reason why presence is important. Being in a state of presence during a session enables a therapist to know whether his client is also becoming more present, what issue to focus on, whether to support or to confront, what course of action to take.

In my trainings, I spend a great deal of time helping participants understand and investigate the state of presence: how to attain it, how to sharpen one's awareness, whether or not one is present, and whether there are any subtle desires or personal agendas that are preventing presence from manifesting. There are many subtle layers of desire in the field of personal growth that can do this; for example, the more one wants to help someone, the more difficult it becomes. Paradoxically, real help happens only when the desire to help has been dropped and, as you can imagine, mastering this art is a delicate process that needs practice and understanding. This does not mean, of course, that one does not do anything, but that action happens as a response to the moment rather than as a deliberate effort to achieve anything.

About Helping

To help, or be helped, is a natural human condition. As social beings, we are all in some way dependent on others, as others depend on us. Or, to put it another way, we live in a state of inter-dependence. There is a process of giving and receiving, which is a fundamental aspect of any relationship, and our readiness to show our need to receive from others creates a basis for exchange.

When we have received, we also feel a certain obligation to return something and in this way an exchange between two people is driven by an underlying force that seeks balance. As a relationship between adults develops, the drive for balance creates a momentum that gradually enriches the exchange between them. In an unequal relationship, such as between parents and children, where children cannot balance what they receive, the drive for balance does not disappear, but creates a slowly building momentum that eventually makes a child leave his parents; his impulse to give is then directed towards others, often to his own children.

In the therapist-client relationship there is also a process of giving and taking, and a therapist should understand that a certain balance needs to be maintained. For example, if a therapist gives too much, perhaps by making himself too available to a client, or by extending the session time over a reasonable limit, he disturbs the relationship. Similarly, what he charges for his work should be in a balanced relation to his expertise, experience and the agreed session time.

Often, therapists and other people in helping professions put themselves in the position of the client's parents and treat the client like a child in need; they feel obliged to pour their compassion on the client almost without limit. In this way, they create a dependency in the client which may eventually create an angry reaction, which in turn may leave the helper perplexed, because he feels he has been giving so much and does not deserve such 'ingratitude.'

This phenomenon has been described as the 'helper syndrome' and is driven by a helper's own need to be needed. By being a helper to others, this type of person can remain unaware of his or her own dependency and need for appreciation. This can create an unhealthy long-term therapist–client relationship in which both partners are equally dependant on the other. Helpers who suffer from exhaustion and burn-out often fall in this category.

Deeper Motives for Helping

There are many ways to examine the deeper motivations of people who want to help others, and the approach of Family Constellation is one of them. Without going into too much description of this particular method, let's look, say, at a helper who wants to save his client from a certain tendency; it could be anything: moods of suicidal depression, addiction to alcohol or drugs, attraction to violent or abusive love partners.... We are not so much concerned here with the nature of the problem as the impulse to help.

When one examines the motivation of this helper through the lens of unfinished family business, one may well discover the feeling of a child who wants to save one of his parents from suffering. Just like the child who cannot stand to see his own parents in misery and wants to save them, now, as an adult therapist, he wants to save his client from suffering. In some instances, this kind of motivation can be the deeper reason why someone chooses to become a therapist in the first place.

However, to be of real help, a therapist has to have the ability to tolerate his client's suffering and resist the temptation to 'save' the client. Then a different kind of help becomes possible. Again, seen from the perspective of Family Constellation, real giving has to be preceded by the experience of receiving, because it is receiving that creates strength in us as individuals and generates the power for us to give to others. This means that a therapist needs to be in a 'right' relation to his own parents, because this is where our original strength came from: when we were children, we grew in strength by receiving from our parents. So, naturally, it is important that a therapist explores, understands and heals his own psychological history, in order to arrive at a state where giving can happen from strength, without hidden needs, personal agendas and expectations.

When the helper is in his strength, he will be aware if his help is really needed, or whether it is inappropriate to give at this moment; whether or not he has the right to help. He is aware of the limits of helping. In other words, a skilled therapist will be able to see the client in his total life context, and will respond to that, rather than operating from theories or beliefs about what will be beneficial. His action will be immediate and will arise out of direct observation of the client's need.

In other words, a client's social, economic and political life situation needs to be taken into account and determines the kind of help that is appropriate. For example, the real need of a client who is living in a conflict zone may be something very different than psychological counseling, or the counseling may need to be different than the usual approach.

Basic Principles

There are a few basic principles here to be understood:

1. A helper can only give what he has. He needs to be sincere and

what he shares must come from his own experience, not just from knowledge.

2. Helping happens in a certain situation and context, which sets boundaries, and a therapist should be sensitive to these limitations, giving what is appropriate and refraining from giving too much. For example, he needs to recognize that he cannot rid a client of the pain of losing a loved one, or the pain of living in poor economic conditions, or in an area of political unrest. At the most, he can help this kind of client become more integrated and find the right steps to deal with this life situation in an appropriate way. The therapist stays in his strength and allows the client to develop his own strength, which often comes by letting him deal fully with a life situation rather than feeling sorry for him.

3. A helper does not put himself in place of his client's parents or allow his client to put him there. He does not help like a parent, nor does he allow a client to demand this kind of help. Rather, he supports a client to remain independent, so there is less opportunity for the phenomenon of transference, in which the client may unconsciously redirect feelings he had towards his parents onto the therapist. Similarly, there is less possibility of counter-transference, in which therapist does the same towards the client. By not remaining stuck in the transference and counter- transference dynamic, a client is ultimately encouraged to separate from his therapist, as well as from his parents, which is what personal growth and maturity is all about.

The Therapist as a Friend

Bert Hellinger, the founder of Family Constellation, put it like this: "When one wants to remain long either in an inferior or superior position, or even searches it, one refuses to take his place as an equal amongst adults."

In classical psychoanalysis, transference is encouraged as a necessary stage of a client's treatment, but in the approach to general counseling outlined in this book the emphasis is slightly different. It may be appropriate to take a parent's position for a short time in order to heal, for example, an attachment problem between a client and his mother. But it is important to keep in mind that the therapist is only representing a parent for a limited period and is not assuming the role of being a 'better parent.' Therefore, the client does not need to separate himself from the therapist, as no state of dependence is allowed to develop. In other words, a helper meets a client, adult to adult, and refuses to be placed in the parent position.

In a deeper sense, a therapist is more like a friend, who accompanies the client. He may be one step ahead, in the sense that the therapist may already know whatever the client is beginning to understand about himself, but it is a temporary situation and concerns only a specific issue, not the whole person. It is important to remember that, as therapists or helpers, we come to know only a tiny fragment about a client and his life circumstances. Moreover, whatever insight a therapist shares with his client is in a certain sense already known by the client's higher self. That is why he can recognize and accept it. It is more like a reminder than an instruction.

Accepting the Rejected

If it is going to be in the service of supporting personal growth, any work done by a counselor or therapist will be searching for what has been rejected by the client and will help him open up to that. Growth is always about including and accepting something inside one's heart that was previously excluded, denied, rejected or suppressed. Whether it is a rejected person, or a denied trauma, or a suppressed emotion, the principle is the same: the helper stands on the side of whatever has been rejected and, in this way, he is doing something that the client still needs to achieve.

In addition, growth is always a movement that takes us beyond judgment, or any moral evaluation, and any help worthy of the name will support this basic principle. This usually means that a therapist does not side with the client's view or standpoint.

The Art of Observation

As described earlier in the book, it is watchfulness that takes us out of identification with the mind. All real help is connected with observation or watchfulness and it is important to understand that this is not the same as thinking and analysis. Thinking tends to take us in circles and nothing radically new is born out of it. At the most, it presents us with a new interpretation of old information. Real insights are born out of direct observation, and the art of direct observation comes from presence, without intention or plan, without fear or prejudice.

In a session, this kind of observation by a therapist leads him to action, but the action is brief and stays with what is essential. It reveals the next step, nothing more, and after the next step has shown itself the therapist withdraws from intervention. In this way, he remains centered within himself and leaves the other alone and in freedom.

Many times, what a therapist observes during a session may be new or surprising to him as well as to the client, and he needs to be free of dogma and theory in order to act upon such observation. By belonging to a certain school of psychology, for example, a therapist's vision will be confined to what is considered relevant or irrelevant by that school. There are many classic examples of how new and diverting discoveries in the development of psychology led to the exclusion of that person from a traditional school. The examples of Jung, Adler and Reich, who came in conflict with Freud, can be listed here.

In my trainings, I emphasize practicing to become aware of the difference between simple observation and theoretical interpretation, a practice which seems to be more difficult for professionals who have already subscribed to a certain approach to psychology and who therefore tend to interpret what they see according to their previous learning. What is required by everyone is an open, unprejudiced mind. Then one can become a medium for a greater force, where the therapist is learning as much from a session as his client. This is the way real insights arrive.

Chapter Thirteen

The Helper-Client Relationship

In this chapter we continue to examine the kind of relating that takes place between a therapist and his client. It is a one-sided relationship in the sense that the therapist does not really share himself, but functions as a mirror for the client. His art is to remain in a state of detachment where there is no personal reaction to anything the client is saying. Instead, the therapist responds to each moment, out of a state of presence, and in this way reflects a deeper truth back to the client.

The less a therapist is personally involved with his client the more effectively he can provide an objective mirror. If there is no personal relationship, it is easier to have no investment or personal opinion, and similarly for a therapist to want anything from a client is a kind of disturbance in a session, contrary to being present and mirroring.

Many therapists are too focused on trying to create and maintain a personal connection and are unaware that this puts a subtle pressure on their clients. Rather than allowing each moment to be as it is and accepting that in a session there are moments of contact and moments of no contact, they make an effort to 'meet' their clients, which, as we saw in the previous chapter, may be rooted in unconscious motivations.

To really be of help, a counselor or therapist needs to have deeply explored his motivation for doing this kind of work. If it comes from a need to be needed, or from the need of having contact, then it will not be of much benefit to the client. A helper may be more in need of his clients than the clients are in need of him.

The need to be needed is one of the most common needs of

human beings and, as I mentioned earlier, has its origins in a child's need to be cared for and loved by his mother. If this need in a therapist has not been fulfilled, he will not be able to deal with the needs of his client in a right way, but will instead try to receive love from a client by winning his admiration and appreciation. To do this, he will be sensing what his client wants and then trying to fulfill these expectations, in this way gaining his client's approval. He will be more a follower of his client than a helper who gives guidance from a state of detachment.

Sexual Manipulation

Any personal desire on the side of the therapist will create disturbance in the session. It may be the desire for love and appreciation, it may be the desire for sex, it may be the desire to be successful and convince the client to come back for more sessions. A therapist must therefore have sufficiently explored his own psychology to be able to stay clear of unconscious desires manifesting in his sessions.

For example, if a therapist has suppressed his sexuality and has not investigated his own issues in this area, it will be difficult for him to support a client to explore sexually-related issues, especially if the client is a member of the opposite sex. He will not be relaxed and comfortable with the subject, or, alternatively, he may use the opportunity to sexually manipulate his client. There are many cases where clients have been exploited sexually by their therapists, in spite of the fact that any kind of sexual relation after a therapy session is bound to be a misuse of power, even if the client agrees to it. The therapist is taking advantage of the special position of authority he has adopted during the session in order to satisfy his personal desires.

In response to this situation, many schools of psychotherapy have developed strict codes of ethical conduct for their members, which is helpful, but which can also be taken to absurd extremes. For example, I heard the story of one therapist who, after ending a series of sessions with a female client, accepted an invitation to her wedding and was promptly threatened with expulsion by his association. Such over-reaction illustrates a deep-rooted fear in many therapists, especially in the United States, where a cultural atmosphere of puritan morality requires hyper-sensitivity on sexual issues, as well as creating a good deal of hypocrisy, and where many therapists get sued by their clients.

In 1991, the award-winning movie *The Prince of Tides* drew protests from a number of US psychiatric associations because of the steamy love affair between the movie's central character, Tom Wingo, played by Nick Nolte, and Dr. Susan Lowenstein, a New York psychiatrist played by Barbara Streisand, who also directed the film. Tom Wingo wasn't even Dr. Lowenstein's patient; he was the brother of a suicidally-depressed woman being treated by Lowenstein, but even this degree of closeness, in a purely fictional drama, was considered enough to require a public protest.

It is a reflection of the immature nature of our social development as sexual beings that, rather than trusting the individual therapist's own understanding, there have to be rules as a way of safeguarding clients from exploitation.

In my view, a therapist-client relationship is a contract for a specific, limited time and the one-sidedness should be dissolved once the work is finished, after which any relating can be part of a wider friendliness. This is possible when the therapist is aware that he functioned as a vehicle for a greater force and that in his own personal life he may not be beyond those problems with which he has helped his client. Any sense of superiority is dissolved because both therapist and client have been able to learn something through their inter-action. By acknowledging this, they part with gratitude.

Responding as a Therapist
It is helpful for both therapist and client to keep in mind that their relationship is artificial, in the sense that a therapist excludes his

own personality and his own issues from the inter-action. For this reason, it is easy for a client to idealize him and imagine he is beyond the kind of problems from which the client is suffering. So a therapist needs to remind himself and sometimes admit to his client that in his own life he is facing similar issues and challenges. Such honesty can help to create an atmosphere of trust, especially when a therapist explains the distinction between what is his personal experience and what is his expertise.

Nevertheless, clients often project a parental figure onto a therapist, expecting the therapist to tell them what to do, or to rescue them from their personal problems, and it is surprising how many therapists fall into this trap, in spite of the fact that such advice is rarely acted upon.

Almost without exception, clients never follow the advice of their therapists, or, if they do, it is not for long. Superficially, they may behave like a 'camel' and say "Yes, you are right and I will try my best," but eventually they become the 'lion' in an unconscious reflex to reassert their own dignity by showing the therapist that his advice didn't work. Then they may seek advice from another therapist and start the whole game again.

Five Ways to Avoid 'Parenting'

How to avoid taking the parental position as a therapist?

To pose the same question in a different way: how not to allow the client to determine and control the inter-action in this way?

The answer is found when we refer back to the discussion of the camel, lion and child archetypes presented in chapter six. The therapist needs to practice being in the space of the child, which means that any action in a session should arise as a spontaneous response to the client and be free of habitual behavior patterns. Since a response from the child state is spontaneous, we cannot establish exact guidelines about *how* to do it, but we can consider examples and hints that point us in the right direction.

Here is an expanded version of the five hints to find presence that were described in chapter three:

1. After a client has raised a question, it is often helpful to allow a gap and not answer immediately. The rhythm of the session, which means the rhythm of the interaction between therapist and client, has to be set by the therapist, which means that if a client is agitated and speedy, the therapist may need to respond by deliberately slowing down. In this way, he balances the energy of the client.

2. The therapist does not need to answer what the client has asked. He may need to ignore the social convention that not answering someone's question is impolite. He may talk about something totally different, if that is what he considers to be the best way of proceeding. Or, rather than answering, the therapist may bring the client's awareness to why he asked the question, or what was his intention in asking it.

3. A therapist needs to be aware of the body position and body language of his client, as this may be more revealing than what is being said. A client may be saying 'yes' while at the same time shaking his head; he may be smiling while at the same time unconsciously making fists with his hands. Also, some clients have a tendency to try and grip the attention of a therapist through strong eye contact, almost like hypnosis, in which case there is no need for the therapist to maintain continuous eye contact.

4. If a therapist asks a question or makes a suggestion, he should not give up when a client does not immediately respond. If the therapist feels a strong impulse to pursue a certain direction in the session, or probe with a certain question, it may be worth seeking a response at least three times before dropping the subject — but not more than that.

5. It is sometimes helpful to respond to a client in a paradoxical way, meaning, a way which the client's mind cannot anticipate

and which therefore leaves him blank. Several famous therapists, including Milton Ericson, were masters of this approach to therapy, and, in a slightly different context, the Zen tradition is full of paradoxical interventions designed to throw a student out of a linear or logical stream of thinking into a direct experience of himself. Jokes have a similar effect, since they begin by creating a certain focus for the mind and then suddenly change everything through an unexpected twist, triggering a release through laughter.

One example of Ericson's gift in this field occurred when he was presented with a 'problem' patient who insisted that he was Jesus Christ. Ericson's immediate response was, "Oh you must be a great carpenter!" and sent him off to the woodworking department of the institution, where he soon began to show signs of reverting to his own identity.

The Responsibility of a Client

Generally speaking, the best way for a therapist to maintain control over a session is to make sure that he does not have an agenda or goal; he does not desire a particular outcome; he does not tell the client what he should or should not be doing. The therapist needs to resist any of these tendencies, even though this is the exact opposite of the common understanding of what 'help' is supposed to be. Rather than carrying a responsibility for the client, he leaves all responsibility to him, including responsibility for the outcome of the session.

Here, it is important to remember that a session works only if a client really wants help and wants it from this particular therapist. It is especially important to clearly establish a client's commitment to a session if he has been sent by some other authority, such as a state institution, where clients are sometimes required to seek counseling in order to receive further benefits, and also in cases where someone else pays for the session, such as a parent or spouse.

'Difficult Clients'

Clients are usually called 'difficult' when a therapist is unable to deal with them, but it is a relative term that often points more towards a therapist's inability and lack of skill than to a defect in a particular client. However, there are clients who insistently focus their energy on creating a certain relationship with a therapist instead of exploring their own issues.

This is a kind of defense mechanism, or, in some cases, it can be a client's way to test his therapist to make sure that he can trust him before becoming vulnerable and exposing psychological wounds. This kind of strategy usually happens in an unconscious way and psychoanalysis has researched the area profoundly.

Some common examples are:

- A client tells a therapist what he wants from him and then expects him to do exactly as imagined, thus trying to control the session.
- A client starts to attack or question the therapist's credibility.
- A woman behaves seductively towards a male therapist in order to control him.
- A client is very resistant and keeps on saying 'no' to whatever the therapist proposes.
- There is also the typically 'good' client who tries in every way to please the therapist, also as a way of controlling the session.

A helpful way to respond to such clients is to wait for a pause in the client's effort to manipulate, which is bound to happen, because to act in such ways is tiring. When there is a slight gap, the therapist acts in that moment, taking care to immediately return afterwards to his state of restfulness. After doing this a few times, a client is usually diverted from his compulsive behavior pattern.

Whatever the situation, it is a challenge for any therapist to remain centered, without reacting and without trying to manipulate the other in return. A typical mistake would be to react as 'camel,' which means the therapist tries to fulfill the client's expectations and demands, or, alternatively, to become a 'lion' and become defensive, authoritative, struggling for control and trying to over-power the client in some way.

It is important to remember that when one finds oneself *trying* to be centered, or *trying* to be in control, this indicates that the therapist's self-connection is already lost. Then it is better to simply acknowledge the situation as it is. By not worrying about a client controlling the session and letting it happen, the therapist remains in charge.

Becoming aware of having lost self-connection is the only way to come out of it. Then one simply disconnects from the client and starts the session afresh, as if nothing has happened before. The therapist should not try to correct what happened before, when he lost control; those moments are passed and nothing can be done about them, or needs to be done about them.

Clients who are experienced as 'difficult' usually prove to be a good learning lesson for a therapist. Sessions that go smoothly will support a therapist's self-confidence, but he will not learn so much from them, in fact he may even become too sure of himself. Sessions that do not go well may not benefit the client as much, but they will certainly benefit the therapist. If nothing else, he will learn modesty.

Taking Oneself Less Seriously

Finally, we need to mention the importance of not being over-identified with a certain method of therapy. It is good to remember that all therapeutic approaches are models that reflect reality only to a limited degree and there is always the possibility that by adhering too closely to a fixed ideology we are missing something important.

Moreover, too much faith in a particular psycho-therapeutic model tends to create a certain arrogance or over-confidence, which in turn is likely to project a pre-conceived diagnosis on a client rather than seeing him as he really is. A therapist who is a little less sure of himself is more likely to be grounded in reality and connected to his own ordinariness. Any dogmatism should be avoided and one's approach should be more light-hearted and less serious.

Just as identification is the main reason for a client's problems, the same is true for a therapist's identification with his way of working. To come out of identification is one of the main pathways for all healing and to be less serious is a sign of a therapist's ability to distance himself from the tools of his trade.

However, the fact that a therapist takes himself lightly does not mean that he dismisses a client's problems or makes light of a client's suffering. On the contrary, this approach will allow the therapist to be more open, receptive and sincere in his relating to his clients. Sometimes, all a client may need for healing is to be received, listened to, acknowledged, loved and taken seriously.

Parable of the Flies

To end the chapter on a humorous note, it is worth recounting this anecdote, taken from one of Osho's discourses, concerning a young man who was convinced that he had swallowed two flies that were continually buzzing around inside his body and would give him no peace. In some respects, the situation mirrors the work of a therapist, since many of the problems with which we are dealing have no existential reality beyond the fact that a client believes them to be real.

Once, a teenage boy was brought to Osho by his parents, who were desperate to solve a certain problem the boy had developed. He imagined that he had swallowed two flies that were now in his stomach and continuously disturbing him. He complained that they were flying everywhere inside his body and driving him crazy, also in the night, so that he could not sleep.

Everyone tried to persuade him that there were no flies inside him, and in desperation the parents had also taken him to doctors and psychiatrists, who examined him, found nothing, and tried to convince him that it was all his imagination... that any fly, if swallowed, would die immediately, and that therefore no flies could possibly be buzzing around inside his body.

But the boy kept insisting about the flies, although nobody believed him.

Finally the parents brought the boy to Osho, who immediately said "Yes, the boy is right. I can see the flies are there inside him."

The parents were shocked, but the boy was very happy, saying "You are the first person who understands me. All those doctors are idiots."

Osho offered to get rid of the flies and when the boy agreed, he blindfolded him, lay him down on a couch and gave him a special mantra to recite. Then he quickly went around the house and caught two flies, put them in a bottle and went back to the boy.

He instructed the boy to open his mouth and report when the flies were flying close to the top of his throat, so Osho could catch them. The boy did so, and Osho acted as if he was grabbing the two flies and capturing them.

Finally, he took off the blindfold from the boy's eyes and showed him the two flies in the bottle. The boy was both impressed and relieved, saying "Those two small flies created such a nightmare for me. Now I will take the bottle and show them to all those who did not believe me."

The boy was cured and his problem did not return.

~

Part Three

Basic Therapeutic Models

In this final section we will compare three therapeutic models of working with people, studying their uniqueness as well as their relative advantages and disadvantages. First, however, there is a general point to be made, which applies to all forms of specialization: as we have previously mentioned, if a therapist specializes in one type of approach he may rise to be a great expert in that field, but the danger is that he may look at all his clients through one particular window that limits his perception.

It is important to remember that it is not the method of therapy itself that primarily helps people, but the understanding and attitude that a skilled therapist brings to a session. In any case, a good therapist will want to familiarize himself with more than one form of therapy, so that he has a bigger 'box of tools' at his disposal, and can spontaneously decide which technique or approach will be more suited to any particular client or situation.

Ultimately, all therapy should aim at expanding consciousness, not just fixing problems, but there are approaches that work more directly on a client's awareness, while others work first on the challenge of getting a person's energy moving. One approach is not necessarily better than the other; everything depends on what is best for this client at this moment.

Therapeutic models also differ in how they gather information and diagnose the problem. This is important, because, generally speaking, the problem a client brings to a session is hardly ever his real problem and so a major part of the work for a therapist is to find the real issue and make an accurate diagnosis.

In general counseling, there is a danger that a therapist will follow a client's own direction too much and rely too much on what is being communicated verbally. In such cases, one may end up having to spend most of the session trying to discover where the real problem lies. To have specific tools and a solid systematic approach can significantly shorten the time one needs to discover the real issue.

The following three models use different methods of gathering relevant information about a client: the first through body behavior, the second through energy reading and the third through family constellation. All three are valid and all three can greatly assist a therapist in his work.

~

Chapter Fourteen

Body-Oriented Approaches and Emotional Awareness

In this chapter we discuss 'Pulsation' as an example of a biodynamic, body-oriented approach to psychotherapy. This type of therapy was pioneered in the 1930s by the brilliant and controversial German psychotherapist, Wilhelm Reich, and then later developed further as a 'Neo-Reichian' tradition, including the works of Alexander Lowen, Gerda Boeysen, Charles Kelley and many others. The name 'Pulsation' has been given more recently by Aneesha Dillon, who was a personal student of Kelley and who learned his 'Radix' approach to Reichian therapy before developing her own personal style. Her new term eloquently expresses Reich's discovery of the 'pulsating' movement found in every life form, which is also reflected in the rhythmic expansion and contraction of the human body as it pulsates with the 'in' and 'out' movement of our breathing.

In Pulsation, the work focuses on the physical body, plus the breath and the movement of energy through the body, which also finds expression in our emotions. The therapist encourages and supports the client to breathe deeply and intervenes in a 'hands on' way, touching and manipulating specific areas of the body to release tension held in the musculature, while at the same time supporting emotional expression and release of mental tension. The underlying concept is that our mind and body are in correlation, reflecting one another, and they can be guided to discharge tension simultaneously in a way that leaves the client feeling both relaxed and energized.

Conditioning and Repression

At the source of the Pulsation approach to therapy is the understanding that our early life conditioning, our social education, deeply affects and often inhibits our body-mind structure. Originally, a newborn child is uninhibited and expresses his natural impulses spontaneously, including the free flow of sexual energy without any attempt to control it. For example, a baby will play openly with his genitals without any sense of shame or embarrassment.

Under natural and normal circumstances, there is a continuous production of energy in our bodies that not only takes care of our daily needs, but also creates a surplus. This is nature's way of ensuring that there is always a reservoir of energy in case of emergencies. Practically speaking, energy starts building at the sex center and also at the 'hara' center in the lower belly, then moves mostly upwards through the body and finds expression and release through the periphery: through the arms, hands, legs, eyes, voice and mouth. One of Reich's most important discoveries was that a full discharge of energy, including the surplus, happens through sexual orgasm and that, without this natural avenue of release, human beings start to become neurotic – we will be looking at the orgasm phenomenon in more detail later in the chapter.

As can be observed in all life forms, there is a natural cycle that promotes health and well-being: energy gathers and builds up to a certain level, at which point it overflows and is expressed and released; then the energy starts to build up again. This cycle has a certain rhythm: the gathering of energy is connected to the in-breath, while the release of energy is connected to the out-breath. In this way, energy 'pulsates,' moving from the center to the periphery and back from the periphery to the center, a rhythm that is reflected in every living organism from a simple amoeba to highly complex, evolved mammals like ourselves.

As a human child grows, this natural pulsation begins to be

inhibited through various methods of social training and conditioning, such as reward and punishment. The child learns that he will be rewarded if he is 'good' and follows the parents' wishes, and will be punished if he is 'bad' and disobeys them. In response to this training he develops a fear of allowing natural impulses and, rather than being expressed, the child's energy gets blocked, or choked; it turns back on itself and a full discharge becomes impossible. Instead, some or all of the charge remains inside the child's bodily tissues, leading to a chronic state of tension that is stored in the body's musculature.

When this happens repeatedly, it leads to the creation of a 'holding pattern' of energy that is locked into our muscles, which become hard and rigid, a process that Wilhelm Reich called 'armoring'. As physical tension and the holding back of emotional expression go hand in hand, one can see how a physiological holding pattern corresponds to an emotional pattern, which is also referred to as a person's 'character.' For example, a person with an angry character usually has a certain body type, as does a fearful person. So character and body type go hand in hand.

This discovery led to the development of schools of psychology that combine body and character types. Alexander Lowen, for example, developed a system that enables a therapist to draw certain conclusions about a client's behavior and emotional attitudes by analyzing the basic structure of his physical body. Pulsation therapists operate with a similar understanding and are able to 'read' clients in this way.

The Three-Layer Personality Model

According to Psychoanalysis and other psychological systems, the mind can be divided into three basic layers: the unconscious mind, the conscious mind and the super-conscious mind, which are stacked on top of each other, rather like the stories of a house. These basic layers can be further sub-divided, but in order to keep things simple we will remain with three. It should also be understood that these divisions are, in a sense, arbitrary, since the hardware of the human brain is not divided in this way, but nevertheless it is a useful method of understanding how our minds work.

The super-conscious is ruled by the super-ego, which is a kind of built-in priest, schoolteacher, judge and censor, all rolled into one. Whatever the super ego judges as 'bad' gets suppressed and is pushed from the conscious to the unconscious layer of the mind. In this way, the super-ego tries to pretend that the rejected element of personality no longer exists, but in reality it does not totally disappear; it is merely hidden from conscious view and continues to function in an indirect yet powerful way from the unconscious.

So the personality is a bit like the layers of an onion, where the deeper layers are hidden in the unconscious, suppressed by the upper layers in an attempt to prevent them from being seen. However, this 'burial' is largely unsuccessful and has serious side-effects. For example, many people are taught to repress their sexual feelings, but sex, as we all know, is an extremely powerful energy. Direct expression may be blocked, but the same energy will sooner or later manifest in more perverted forms, such as an interest in pornography, or visits to prostitutes, or child abuse, or, conversely, as a kind of angry virtue that seeks to impose moral restrictions on others... and so on.

This perversion of natural expression becomes visible at a collective level when, for example, the general public becomes fascinated with the sex lives of famous people. The American public's appetite for the intimate details of the love affair between President Bill Clinton and Monica Lewinsky, and the British public's eagerness to hear tape recordings of Princess Diana talking to one of her lovers, are both symptoms of sexual repression.

The Social Mask

The conscious layer of the mind is generally interpreted as positive and contains our 'normal' social behavior. This is the first level, where, for example, we present a superficially friendly attitude to the world, acting as if everything is okay, listening politely to others, hiding what we are really thinking…. It is a false social face that we show to each other and it functions as a civilizing lubricant so that we can all get along together without too much discord or conflict.

There are generally agreed rules for this social game. For example, when the check-out clerk at the supermarket smiles pleasantly and says "Hi, how are you today?" we know that we are not being invited to pour out our problems; we just smile back, say "fine, thanks," pay the bill and head for the door. We also try not to get into a shouting match with a love partner in a public setting; we would much rather present the appearance of being devoted to each other so that other people will accept and admire us as a couple.

Anything that is socially unacceptable — in other words whatever is judged by the super-ego as 'wrong' — gets suppressed into the second layer, which is more or less unconscious. This process of suppression starts early. As children, we are told many times "Don't cry… don't be angry… don't be so loud… don't touch yourself there…." We soon learn to have negative attitudes towards all of these impulses, gradually understanding that they are bad and must be hidden, and so the second layer is usually full of negativity. It is a bit like a garbage bin that gets steadily bigger and bigger as we grow up.

However, our control over the first layer is fragile and can wear off quickly, exposing the negativity underneath. When this happens, we may discover that the second layer is very thick and holds all that we have suppressed during our lives. This is the reason why we are afraid to come in touch with the second layer, because it seems so strong and powerful, and also because we realize that if we allow it to be expressed it will bring us into conflict with society. As we all know, trying to emptying a garbage bin is not a pleasant experience.

Pulsation acknowledges that it is the body that suffers most from the process of social conditioning, because its natural impulses are condemned and suppressed, especially its sexual impulses. Pulsation and other body-oriented approaches guide and encourage the body to return to its natural state by using a variety of methods to release held-back and suppressed energy. This means that a Pulsation client has to pass through and empty the content of the second layer, allowing its negativity to be exposed and expressed.

Once the natural state has been regained, energy begins to flow freely through the body and this is usually accompanied by positive feelings that are far more authentic than the superficial social façade that was hiding the second layer. Here, one experiences a relaxed and innocent state of well-being, perhaps for the first time since childhood, plus a sensation of pulsating aliveness, joy and enthusiasm for life. This is sometimes referred to as the third layer, but it should not be confused with the super-conscious. It is, in reality, a new and fresh experience of the conscious layer that has now been freed of both the super-ego and the unconscious repressions that were inhibiting its natural state.

The De-Conditioning Process

As we have already mentioned, energy has an outward and an inward impulse; it expands and reaches out, then withdraws and contracts, and this 'pulsation' is the essential rhythm of all life. In human beings, energy becomes inhibited during the conditioning process, either on the outward stroke, or the inward stroke, or both, and the work of a Pulsation therapist consists mainly of helping this inhibited energy to find some kind of completion and regain its natural, healthy rhythm.

This is achieved through deep breathing, especially through

breathing down into the belly, as this is where we connect with our life energy. Of course, in anatomical terms, we cannot breathe into the belly, only into the lungs, but deep breathing has the effect of pushing the diaphragm downwards, which in turn pushes the belly out – this is what we mean by belly breathing.

Belly breathing functions as the medium that connects us to denied emotions and feelings that have been stored in the body's tissues, frozen in our musculature. Whatever has been repressed begins to surface and comes to the attention of the conscious mind.

The therapist supports this process through touch and through guiding and encouraging a person with his voice, while the client is lying on a mat, on his back, breathing deeply with an open mouth. He also encourages the client to move his body in ways that can help to 'unfreeze' those areas where energy has become stuck.

Most of our suppressed emotions are negative, so the deep breathing soon begins to touch layers of anger, hate, pain and fear. However, we also have repressed positive energies like love and sex, and these, too, begin to surface. In Pulsation, the 'de-armoring' process usually starts at the periphery, which means at the extremities – arms, legs and head — then gradually penetrates to the core parts of the body, like the belly and pelvis, where our more deep-seated feelings originate.

This layer-by-layer approach goes back to Reich, who discovered that the body has a segmental structure, similar to that of primitive life forms. A worm, for example, has a series of muscular rings, or sphincter muscles, that surround a central tube and it is through the rhythmic contraction and expansion of these rings that a worm moves and digests its food. Similarly, Reich understood that human energy moves through a series of body segments, supported by rhythmic contractions that also occur in the orgasm reflex.

A comprehensive description of the different segments and

how a Pulsation facilitator works with them is given by Aneesha Dillon in her book *Tantric Pulsation* and is not required here. What is important to understand is that the main intention of this work is to re-establish the natural rhythm of the pulsating movement through all of these segments, especially those that have become frozen or inhibited through life-long conditioning. In this process, a therapist may have to deal with a 'counter-pulsation' movement in the client, which originates from a child's attempt to push down impulses that he has learned are 'bad' and therefore painful.

The Pulsation process can also be seen as an inter-play between saying 'no' and saying 'yes.' In most Reichian and Neo-Reichian therapies, the facilitator supports a client to allow his 'no' to be expressed, sometimes in a cathartic way, and this helps to unfreeze the stuck energy so that the client's natural pulsation can be restored, which is, in effect, saying 'yes' to his own life energy and celebrating it.

The art of working with this approach, as well as other cathartic therapies like Primal, is to help a client reach the positive layer, to learn to say 'yes' to himself rather than remaining in reaction and expressing only the negative.

The Orgasm Formula

A few words need to be said about Reich's Orgasm Formula, which demonstrates the principle of how energy moves. Before energy can become dynamic and expressive, it needs to go through a phase where a charge is built up, and this can be illustrated through the example of sexual attraction that happens between a man and a woman.

When a man and woman are attracted to one another and begin to move closer to each other, they experience what we call a growing 'charge' of energy. They may feel it as body heat, or as a kind of electricity in the way they touch, or a sense of excitement, an accelerated heartbeat, heightened mental awareness, perspiration... many different sensations that indicate a general build-up of energy.

As the energy level increases there is also a growing feeling of tension: on the one hand the man and woman want to contain the energy charge, on the other hand they look for ways to release it. As they move into sexual embrace, passing through foreplay and into love-making, the overall energy level increases more and more, eventually reaching a point where it becomes too difficult to contain and a sudden discharge occurs, which is then followed by a feeling of relief and deep relaxation.

In case of a sexual meeting, this is called 'orgasm' and one of its characteristics is that it remains voluntary, in our control, only up to a certain point, while beyond this 'point of no return' it becomes involuntary. When the point of no return is reached, the body goes into a series of involuntary convulsions – if it is allowed to follow its natural pattern – while at the same time streams of bio-electricity flow strongly through the body's tissues as it discharges accumulated energy and tension. The more a person can let go of control in the moment of orgasm and allow these involuntary movements, the more fully the energy discharges and the deeper the state of relaxation and well-being that follows.

In his studies of orgasm, Reich asserts that for a person to be able to allow the involuntary stage of orgasm is a sign of physical and psychological health. The Pulsation process embraces a similar understanding: a client is guided into deep breathing in order to build up a charge of energy that is used to connect with repressed feelings, which are then discharged in an expressive release of emotional energy. Part of the therapist's job is to help a client build a charge while containing the energy so that release does not happen prematurely and a powerful charge can be created. At a certain point, the growing level of energy in the body will begin to highlight tense areas in the musculature and the therapist will probably focus on one of these areas, using touch and pressure to trigger the discharge of emotions that have been held back.

This is a simple description of the basic principle of Pulsation and, indeed, of most cathartic therapy work. We will now examine some of the benefits and practical points to be considered when working with breathing and emotional release.

The Wisdom of the Body

We saw in the beginning of this book that the ability to feel and sense one's own physical body is an important and necessary step towards finding one's true nature. As Osho puts it in one of his discourses: "All growth depends on how one is related to one's body…. If you have not explored your body, you will not be able to explore the soul." In other words, a healthy relationship to the body and respect for its functioning is a must for any kind of personal integration, because whatever we experience and whatever we think has an impact on the body.

It follows that all therapeutic work has to include the body to a certain degree, and the benefit of a body-oriented approach like Pulsation is that, from the very beginning, it operates on a bodily level. It helps a person become deeply rooted and connected to the body and its functioning. A client does not need to think about his problems and their possible solutions; he can simply lie down, move into the Pulsation method of deep breathing and trust that whatever is important will reveal itself through a physical, emotional and energetic experience.

This helps a client to be less identified with the mind and its tendency to analyze, interpret and judge whatever is happening. Instead, the mind is invited to focus on the breathing, which is a here-and-now phenomenon that is intimately connected to meditation; this is why Buddhism has used the principle of watching the breath as one of its main approaches to meditation for thousands of years. Through breath, one has the opportunity to be more in touch with the body and with the present moment and, in the world of therapy and counseling, these two qualities are already a big step towards healing.

However, to work only on the level of body and emotion can leave issues unresolved and unclear, and in Neo-Reichian work there is a danger of remaining identified with the formula of charge and discharge without striving for greater awareness. Learning emotional expression can lead to a kind of addiction to being expressive, so that, just as previously one has been addicted to repression, one now becomes addicted to expression. Real transformation is connected to growth in awareness, so that one can respond to any situation from a state of consciousness where one is free to express or not to express. Expressiveness can also be a way of avoiding real feeling; for example, staying safe in the expression of anger while the underlying, hidden feeling is one of vulnerability and fear.

It needs to be remembered that, ultimately, therapy is not about getting rid of our emotions, or even expressing them, but about becoming aware of them, understanding how they operate and how the body is affected. In the initial phase of a client's process, it may be important to scream, shout and express — especially if the client is overcharged with energy and feelings – but later on it will become increasingly meaningful to contain and simply feel whatever is there, without doing anything about it.

A person's body structure may change through Pulsation work, armoring may dissolve, energy flow may be restored, and all this is for the good, but a skilled therapist should help a client go beyond any preoccupation with whether or not such changes occur. It needs to be remembered that the body easily falls into habits and has a tendency to repeat the past, resuming old patterns even after blocked energy has been released. Real transformation must also include understanding and awareness, which are functions of consciousness.

Effortless Effort

Pulsation and other forms of breath work require a client to make an effort to breathe more deeply, in a voluntary way, otherwise nothing is going to happen. But while the client is making this effort the process remains to a certain extent within his control and in this way it is limited. At some point, the client needs to be able to let go of effort and trust whatever his body is doing, or wants to do, by itself. In order to arrive at a deeper level of integration, or insight, he needs to surrender to the impulses of the body and its energy.

Here, problems can arise. For example, a client may be unwilling to make any kind of effort — he may resist the process at a conscious or unconscious level — and then no charge will be built up, so no deep discharge can happen. Or, a client may not be able to let go of control at the point of no return and then the effort he continues to make will actually become a hindrance for anything new to happen.

All new experiences require that we are ready to surrender to something bigger than whatever we think we know, or want. Sometimes, clients have certain ideas about what they want to achieve in a session; for example, to get rid of their anger, or to allow their pain and express it. They may make a comparison with what happened in a previous session, in which case they will not be connected to the present moment, but remain in a state of expectation and goal-orientation. Rather than releasing tension, they may become more tense and this will prevent the release, or discharge.

For these reasons, the necessary effort at the beginning of a session can become a habit that does not allow a person to move ahead and come out of old patterns. In these instances, it is important that the therapist focuses on relaxation, rather than on building up charge, and on making the client aware of the repetitive cycle. This is possible only if the therapist himself is not attached to the technique of releasing emotion, but can see the bigger picture of what is happening to the client.

Balancing the Negative

As already mentioned, a person who goes into deep breathing is often faced with repressed negativity and this can be quite challenging for a client, especially if he is sitting on a volcano of emotions, or has been struggling to keep difficult experiences under control. To be suddenly faced with a lot of negativity may be an overwhelming experience, especially if it is not balanced with the positive state of feeling grounded in one's true being. The situation can be made worse if a person feels pressure, or expectation, from the therapist, or from other participants in a group situation.

People who are suffering from trauma can get re-traumatized when going into a process where deep emotions are being brought to the surface. A cathartic session can reach a point where the person starts to re-live a previous traumatic event, a phenomenon that has been described as entering a 'trauma vortex'. Rather than helping a person to digest and complete the past, this can lead to further aggravation. In cases of dealing with trauma, the therapist should help the client focus on becoming grounded in the body and feeling resourced by positive states. Breath work should be introduced gradually, so the client learns how to feel and sense the body, becoming slowly more comfortable with containing a higher charge.

Repression, Expression and Containment

Osho has repeatedly emphasized that repression is anti-life, it is a kind of suicide whereby we kill our energy and yet somehow continue to drag ourselves through daily life, so the value of methods like Pulsation that reawaken our energy is very significant.

However, one of the problems of cathartic work is that people tend to focus too much on expressive release and too little on learning to contain the energy that is being reawakened. One has to learn how to make the body a stronger container for emotions and energy, and expression can only be a part of this process. Of course, one has to be aware of the difference between containment and control, but controlling one's energy can be judged too negatively, without taking into account those times when control is necessary and needed. For example, a traumatized person has to learn to be in control of himself, rather than being overwhelmed; only then will it become possible to experience relaxation and let go.

A balanced way of working gives space for both expression and containment, and takes into account how fast or how slowly issues can be approached with each individual client. To be on the safe side, it is good to work slowly and to make sure a person feels enough support and trust before entering any issue. Clients who are in a hurry, or who want to force something to happen quickly, are often unaware of their fear and of the feelings they are trying to avoid.

Three Breathing Patterns

The way someone is breathing also reflects his approach to life. In breathing, we take in oxygen and we throw out carbon dioxide, we are receiving life energy and giving out what the body does not need. Each breath is a small charge and discharge. When we breathe in we are allowing ourselves to feel, when we breathe out we are expressing ourselves and letting go.

This process of receiving and giving has been inhibited at both extremes because of our conditioning. As a result, people tend to either not inhale fully, or not exhale fully, or to breathe shallowly in both directions. These inhibited patterns were created during the years of conditioning and are indicative of the way we live and the way we deal with our emotions.

A person who does not exhale fully is preventing the out-moving energy, including emotions like anger, from finding completion. Typically, this kind of person is overcharged with energy at the periphery of the body because the release is not total. Supporting expression is a helpful way to complete the out-going stroke of the breathing pulsation. This can happen through movements of the hands, arms, legs, eyes and jaw, and also through words and sounds.

A person, who does not inhale fully is preventing the in-coming stroke of the breathing pulsation and is therefore not allowing any charge to build, which is why this type of body usually appears under-charged or collapsed. In this case, it will be supportive to help the client come more in touch with his feelings, especially feelings of fear, or terror, and to slowly allow more charge to be contained in the body.

A third pattern is for a person to neither inhale fully, nor exhale fully, and to contain a lot of charge at the core of the body. This type of person usually has a compact body and it will be helpful to support a full in-and-out breath, which may evoke feelings of pain, so that both strokes of the pulsation can be deepened and find completion.

These three patterns relate to specific body types and the blocking of particular emotions, and any insight that a client gains through deep breathing will require an awareness of his basic pattern so that it can be dissolved.

To conclude: one should use the breath to become more conscious of the present moment; whether this moment brings any emotional release is secondary. The focus should remain on the breathing and not on what is coming to the surface in terms of emotional energy. The breathing functions as a guide and so an awareness of the breathing should be kept at all times.

Some doing and some effort will be required from the client, but it should be a 'relaxed effort' that is not trying to force a release or result. At the same time, the client should be supported in resisting any tendency to give up, because nothing appears to be happening. Avoiding these two extremes, Pulsation and other breath work can become a great adventure of self-discovery.

Example of a Pulsation Session

Wolfgang is a tall man, about 40 years old, with a strong body that is clearly tense in the upper part, around the shoulders and arms. As far as his personality is concerned, he seems to be a rather friendly character and does not have much experience with breath work.

After an initial talk, the therapist asks the client to lie down on his back, with his knees raised and feet flat on the mattress. This is the standard position in Pulsation sessions and has a grounding effect, helping a person stay present and alert, without going to sleep or daydreaming, in which case the legs would fall to one side.

The client is asked to keep his mouth open and start breathing through the mouth in a way that slowly deepens and intensifies, imagining that the breath reaches all the way down to the belly. The focus in the beginning is on the in-breath and the breathing should be continuous and uninterrupted, without leaving long gaps between the in-breath and out-breath. This helps to build a charge of energy in the body and supports the client in getting in touch with his feelings.

The therapist encourages the breathing to go deep by touching the client's belly, gently loosening the muscles. After a while, the touch includes working on the diaphragm, which is one of the most important muscles for breathing and is often inhibited, since one of the most effective ways to block unwanted emotion is to stop breathing. This is why the diaphragm tends to be tight in most people. If it is loosened too quickly, a client can get flooded with emotions, so the therapist's approach is firm, but gentle, without trying to force a quick release, respecting a person's capacity.

In Wolfgang's case, he tends to hold his breath in and this prevents a full out-breath. He also tends to close his mouth, so the therapist also touches his chin, reminding him to keep his mouth wide open.

Wolfgang is asked to slowly increase the depth and intensity of his breathing, without straining and without leaving long gaps. The therapist lightly touches his legs and feet to help him stay in contact with this part of his body. He encourages this further by asking Wolfgang to rock his pelvis in time to his breathing rhythm. In this way, Wolfgang is being asked to do some voluntary movement, which further supports his contact with the lower part of his body, while simultaneously provoking any held-back energy in the pelvic area.

Basically, the therapist is trying to increase the amount of energy that moves through the whole body, which will also begin to highlight any frozen places — places that do not participate in the overall pulsation. This gives an indication to the therapist where to touch and what to support.

As Wolfgang continues to build up a charge of energy in his body, the shoulders, neck and jaw are becoming visibly more and more tight, and the therapist asks him to bring his awareness to these areas and explore various movements to help loosen the tightness. At the same time, the therapist touches the musculature in those areas, also with the purpose of releasing tension.

After a while, Wolfgang is asked to open his eyes and look at the therapist for a moment, as this encourages energy to move out through the eyes, and he is also asked to become aware of any fear that may be stopping his movements, especially the fear of showing anger. In Wolfgang's case, it is the out-going stroke of energy that needs to be supported.

Wolfgang has enough trust and inner stability to enjoy the growing feeling of power, strength and vitality that he experiences as he becomes more and more energetic. As the session develops, he begins to hit the mattress with his fists and stamp his feet, making loud sounds, coming in touch with feelings of anger that he has been holding back. His continuous smile gives way to a more authentic expression.

After each phase of expression, the therapist helps Wolfgang to again focus on the breath, noticing his enhanced breathing capacity and expansion of inner space. Through touch and verbal guidance he helps him to remain in contact with his body and breath, present to any experience that arises in the moment, including any memories from the past.

In this way, Wolfgang moves through cycles of charge and discharge, during which his experience of strength and integrity steadily grows, increasing his overall vitality. Throughout the work, the focus remains on the breathing.

After the completion of a third cycle, the therapist helps his client relax and before ending the session gives time for integration, allowing Wolfgang to 'ground' his new sense of strength and vitality in his whole body. Through his bodily experiences, Wolfgang has become more aware of his tendency to hold himself back while relating with others, asking for people's approval and thereby compromising his energy, which in turn leads to emotional and physical tension.

At the end of this session, he can sense that he has the capacity and strength to enjoy his energy by himself, which will make him less dependent on seeking approval from others, and less willing to put on a 'nice' facade. He is discovering how to really enjoy himself. A key insight was to see how he was not allowing himself to feel the negative side of his energy — like anger for example – and how this blocked energy was in turn preventing him from allowing authentic positive feelings like love.

This is just one example of how the Pulsation method helps to give a client a sense of inner expansion and well-being, using the basic method of charge and discharge to unblock and release stagnant energy, restoring the body's natural rhythm.

Chapter Fifteen

Energy Work

In energy work a therapist does not approach a 'problem' directly, but in a more indirect way. While a Pulsation therapist may focus on a tense area in the body and try to release the held-back energy, in this type of work the focus is to support and nourish energy that is already healthy and flowing. The idea is that, by giving attention to existing states of well-being, a client can be reminded about that which is already healthy in him and this can create a new orientation towards the positive, which, as a by-product, helps him come out of the problem-oriented tendency of the mind.

In this way, that which is already healthy gets supported and grows, while the negative is seen as something to be recognized and accepted at a certain stage of a person's growth in consciousness — not something that needs to be fought with, but only understood. This view is based on the principle mentioned at the beginning of this book: negative states are only an absence of natural, positive states, just as darkness is only an absence of light. By fighting against negative states, we give them substance and reality.

There may come a moment in this work when the negative is confronted as well, but this happens only with clients who have reached a certain level of maturity and usually not in an early stage of a session. Rather than attacking the ego directly, a major part of the work is to nourish and support a deeper state of being, because the 'ego structure' has no real existence; it is only an absence. For example, if a client wants to get rid of anger, then rather than supporting the release of anger in this person, one would support a feeling of self-love, even in the presence of angry feelings.

In other words, one may support a neglected side of a client, which eventually brings transformation to other parts as a side effect. A similar approach can be adopted with other negative emotions or personality traits: fear can be seen as an absence of trust, pain as the absence of joy, and so on. So the therapeutic approach is focused on building a solid, positive connection to one's essential being, before dealing with any negative issues of the personality.

The American therapist Sagarpriya Delong has developed two types of energy work, Psychic Massage and Star Sapphire, which will serve as models for describing this approach to therapy. In both Psychic Massage and Star Sapphire, the focus from the beginning of a session is to create awareness, without being too concerned about the dynamic movement of energy. So the name 'energy work' may be misleading, as it gives the impression that the therapist is focusing on the state of energy flowing through the client's body, whereas in fact it is a person's consciousness that is being addressed. As we will see, energy and consciousness can be looked at separately.

Consciousness is not a commodity that can be given; it is already inherent within the client, so the work focuses on creating the right atmosphere in which whatever is hidden receives support and spontaneously emerges into the open. The common idea that a client comes to a counseling session with a question, or issue, which the therapist will answer, and then the client will know what to do, is basically wrong. Transformation happens in the form of spontaneous understanding and insight within the client, rather like a personal discovery, so the function of the therapist is that of a midwife, helping the client give birth to a higher state of consciousness.

In this way, an effective session is a shift in dimension, or state, from mind to being, from negative to positive, from looking out to looking inside oneself, from trying to get something 'out there' to accepting and relaxing with what already is the case.

Distinguishing Energy and Consciousness

Any kind of event can be 'seen' or 'witnessed' on the inner screen of our consciousness. It can be an image, a feeling, a sensation, a thought. Meditation is concerned with the ability to watch these events and this ability varies from person to person: one can have a big or small capacity to remain watchful without getting identified with whatever events are being reflected on the inner screen. Personal growth is related to expanding the capacity to witness events and to be able to say 'yes' to them. This is also called acceptance.

For example, a person may feel jealous and be completely identified with this emotion, with no distance and no capacity to watch. A second person may feel jealous, may also be aware of his jealousy, while at the same time strongly disliking this aspect of himself, rejecting it as unacceptable. A third person may feel jealous, be aware of the jealousy, and accept that this is so, without judging himself for it. All three people are having the same experience of jealousy, but the way that each individual relates to the emotion is different.

So a therapist can notice two things in a session: he can feel the client's energy, in this case the energy of jealousy, and he can also sense the client's ability to be conscious, to be in a state of inner 'yes' with what is. In Psychic Massage and Star Sapphire Energy work there is a special word for this ability to be in a state of yes: it is called 'resonance.' As explained in chapter three, by sensing the degree of resonance, a therapist can tell to what extent a client is connected to his own being and how deeply he is identified with his mind. The way the therapist works will differ according to the degree of resonance he finds in each client.

Seven Chakras: Reading Energy and Resonance

In the last chapter, we described how emotions are held in the body and its musculature. In fact, all our past experiences, including thoughts, memories and subtle energies can be accessed through the body. Not only does the body carry different energies, it also can be more alive or less alive, more conscious or less conscious, in different areas. In other words, it can be more or less 'resonant.'

Through developing a method of 'reading' the resonance of a client and his energy, Sagarpriya Delong has found a way to access and understand not only a person's different energies and personality traits, but also a way to discover which parts of the body are more conscious.

A session develops as follows:

After an initial talk, the therapist asks the client to lie down on his back, on a couch, and close his eyes. When the client is comfortable, the therapist holds one hand at a distance of about six inches above the body, in order to read the client's energy and degree of resonance.

The hand is placed above each 'chakra' to read the energy and resonance of each of these centers. As most people know, the concept of chakras originated in India and indicates a series of energy centers in the body that posses certain qualities, each one reflecting a different aspect of a person's energy. The number of chakras varies from five to nine, according to different spiritual systems, but the most common consists of seven:

1. The root chakra, or sex center, at the base of the spine.
2. The feeling chakra, just below the navel.
3. The power chakra, in the solar plexus.
4. The heart chakra, in the middle of the chest.
5. The throat chakra, in the center of the throat.
6. The third eye, between the eyebrows.
7. The crown chakra, at the top of the head.

Whole books have been written about the chakras and their

properties, but this brief explanation will suffice for the purpose of describing energy work as a form of therapy. Through reading the chakras, the therapist obtains a detailed map of the client's energy, feelings, mind-structure and state of consciousness. For example, he can know where the client's body is open and relaxed, where it is in a state of resonance, and what kind of feelings, attitudes or memories are carried in different parts of the body.

This provides useful information for the therapist, in addition to whatever his client told him in the beginning, and helps him decide how to start the session, where to focus, how much support to give, how directly an issue can be addressed and what kind of outcome may be possible at the end of this session.

Initially, this reading is for the purpose of helping the therapist direct his work. However, at some point of the session, the therapist will usually talk to his client about some of the things he has discovered. This is done in response to the client's needs and not in the form of passing on information just for the sake of it.

Four Categories of Potential

Besides reading the individual chakras the therapist also gives a reading of the client's general resonance and energy, which is a bit like gaining an overall impression of a house after looking into its various rooms. In terms of resonance, this will take the form of a quantitative assessment, adding up the readings of the individual chakras. This, in turn, will help the therapist to know when it is helpful to 'disturb' or 'confront' a client, working on the roots of his personality structure, and when it is better to give support and connect him to his inner being.

According to the amount of general resonance, one can place clients in four basic categories: no resonance, little resonance, medium resonance, a lot of resonance. These divisions are to a certain extent arbitrary, as there are no categories in a quantitative continuum, but they are helpful in a practical way.

1. No Resonance.

When the therapist finds no resonance anywhere in the body, including no general resonance, the client belongs to the first category. This usually means that the person has no experience of meditation, is not familiar with being in a relaxed state of 'yes' to the present moment, and is largely unaware of his inner being. The work of the session will be to help the client experience a glimpse of meditation. In this category, a client will have many desires and personality issues, but there will be little or no opportunity to solve them in the session. Rather, the client needs to learn first to be less identified with his problems and experience some well-being, even if his issues are not 'solved.'

2. Little Resonance.

When the therapist finds resonance clearly in at least one chakra and a small amount of general resonance, the client belongs to the second category. This type of person has experienced meditation and can access his inner being, but easily loses the connection when challenged with difficulties. He may be joyful at times, but when a problem appears he moves into the mind and gets lost in worries and tension. While the first type of client needs to be helped to find his being, this client needs support to become more rooted and grounded in his being and in relaxation.

3. Medium Resonance.

In the third category, a client has medium resonance in at least one chakra, some resonance in other chakras and also medium strength general resonance. In this state, the client has one foot in the dimension of desire and one foot in the dimension of being, living in a state of worry and tension for 50 percent of the time, and 50 percent in relaxation and well-being. He can be watchful of himself, but when confronted with difficulties for a sustained period he will become identified with feelings or thoughts, losing his sense of 'who he really is.' Accordingly, any therapeutic work will be 50 percent supportive and 50 percent confrontational: when the client is identified, he will be supported to find contact with his being; when this has happened, the therapist will address issues of the personality. The principle here is similar to the pendulation process described in chapter twelve.

4. A Lot of Resonance.

In the last category, a client has medium resonance in more than one chakra and a high degree of general resonance. This person is able to keep a continuing sense of 'who he really is,' even if situations become difficult and challenging. This is the only case in which a session does not need to start with support, since the client already has a connection to his inner being and is mature enough to stay in contact without assistance. The session can begin by directly focusing on the issue the client has presented.

Degrees of Exploration

According to their potential, these different types of clients will each receive a different type of session, even their issues are similar. For example, if a client's issue is the painful ending of a love relationship, the four scenarios may look like this:

Type One: the therapist focuses on trying to find ways of meeting the client's being where he can experience a glimpse of watchfulness and relaxation. There is no direct 'work' on the issue, as the level of identification is too high, so the learning is about finding distance.

Type Two: the client knows what relaxation feels like, but is continuously drawn into his desire for the other. The therapist keeps reminding the client about areas in his life where he feels fulfillment, maybe helping him to remember that there is still love available even if this particular partner is not with him any longer. He works on establishing more roots in the area of being.

The therapist may acknowledge the pain but will not support the client's desire to get back his lost lover, or enter the sadness of loss more deeply. The work is to resource and support the client, similar to the example given in chapter nine.

Type Three: initially, this client will be supported, just like type two. Then the therapist may confront him by asking him to look at the way in which he contributed to the separation. When he gets too involved and identified, perhaps moving into blame rather than remaining connected to his own feeling, the therapist will leave the issue and focus on resources that help the client remember himself and his ability to take responsibility. The work shifts between support and dealing with issues, as shown in the example in chapter ten.

Type Four: this client is not in need of support and the session can begin by focusing on the issue. As we already said, this type of client is rooted in his being and will be able to keep a sense of watchfulness, even when looking at his pain, his sense of loss, and his behavior patterns in relationships. He may be confronted, to see in what way he is responsible for ending the relationship and look at his own shadow side. Most of the session can be spent examining different aspects of the issue, similar to the example given at the end of this chapter.

Male-Female Polarity
Psychic Massage and Star Sapphire energy work use the model of the inner male and inner female polarity, discussed in chapter eight, as a way to understand the development of personality. As previously mentioned, the body can be seen as being divided down a vertical mid-line, with the left half carrying the female energy and the right half carrying the male energy.

The roots of these energies can be contacted most easily through the left and right legs of the client, and in Psychic

Massage and Star Sapphire work the therapist gives a psychic reading of each leg to determine the resonance and energy of the male and female sides. This is done by holding each foot in turn and is part of the initial reading given at the beginning of a session. In this way, the therapist gains insight into the inner polarity and can decide whether the inner woman or inner man should receive more attention and support.

Usually, one side has more resonance, which means that one side is more spiritually developed than the other. In less resonant clients, it is often the case that the less resonant side is the cause of difficulties, such as, for example, feeling superior and dominating the other side. The more resonant side needs to be supported to grow in strength in order to stand up for himself, or herself. In more resonant clients, the more resonant side can be the cause of the problem, for example, by judging the less mature side and not allowing it to have its own space. This can be the result of a so called 'spiritual' ego that needs to be confronted in a session. These are general examples; it needs to be remembered that each case is different and needs to be individually examined – examples were given in chapters seven and eight.

While Psychic Massage works on the inner man-woman polarity mainly through massage and touch, with some talking towards the end of the session, Star Sapphire work uses the Gestalt model that has already been described, allowing the male and female to come into the open and communicate with each other. Here, the inner man and inner woman are treated like two partners in a relationship session, where the work consists in helping each side find his or her unique expression and strength.

Conditioning and Resonance

Conditioning is understood as a process in which different aspects of a person's psyche get rejected, suppressed or isolated. This rejection is a result of the ideals and beliefs we have been given by society, telling us how we should behave. If we come across an expression of our own energy — anger, sensuality, sadness, or joy, for example — that is not acceptable in terms of these ideals, we start rejecting it, while at the same time trying to imitate whatever behavior we have been told is acceptable and desirable. In chapter four, we explained how this leads to hypocrisy and, in chapter fourteen, we described how real feelings are suppressed.

The rejected part of the personality does not disappear, but remains as a disowned energy within us. When a therapist gives an energy reading, he will be able to sense such an energy, depending on how much it has been repressed. Simultaneously, when he checks the level of resonance, he will give a 'no resonance' reading, or at the most will find only slight resonance, depending on the degree to which this part of the body is in a state of 'no' or 'asleep.' Areas of the body where the energy has been accepted and welcomed will be read as 'resonant.' The more fully an area has been accepted, the more resonant it will be. So there are degrees of resonance and of no-resonance.

As a metaphor, one can think of the body in shades of white and black, where 'white' indicates resonance and vitality, while 'black' indicates non-resonance and resistance to life. The white areas are more connected to one's being, while the black areas are more connected to the mind and its conditioning. So, in this model of energy work, growth means an expansion of the resonant or 'white' areas in the body, indicating an expansion of relaxation and self-acceptance.

Re-Learning and Reclaiming

The de-conditioning process in this kind of energy work consists of re-learning and re-claiming energy from the non-resonant to the resonant system. For example, if a client has believed that "I am a nice person, who can give to others without needing anything in return," he may need to learn to listen to a deeper layer of his conscious mind that knows a different truth. In order to be able to listen to this deeper inner voice, which wants to make him aware of his real needs, the client may need to let go of some conditioned ideas, for example that to be 'in need' is weakness and should be avoided.

This work can also be seen in terms of helping an energy return to its natural state, coming out of desire and celebrating what is already the case. In this way any disowned energy is given the chance to transform itself; for example, what appears to a client as 'needy' at the beginning of a session may be experienced later as vulnerability.

In terms of the inner man and inner woman dynamic, it is a learning for each side to settle in aloneness and relax with what is, dropping the hope that the other will fulfill one's desires.

In terms of practical work in a session, much depends on the reading of resonance and understanding the potential of a client, since these are the main indicators for the therapist to decide how to proceed.

There are four basic steps:

1. Finding resonance.
2. Supporting resonance.
3. Expanding resonance.
4. Reclaiming the natural state.

Reclaiming refers to working with non-resonant parts of the personality that are helped to come back to the alive, vibrating, natural state. This does not happen through 'doing' in the ordinary sense, since growth in consciousness and the ceasing of desire is not something that can be 'done;' it is, rather, a by-product of understanding. Therapy helps to prepare the ground for this understanding to flower.

Learning to listen to one's inner voice and follow it does, of course, have immediate and practical consequences in a client's daily life. For example, in a session, it may become clear what the inner man and inner woman enjoy to do in life, what is each one's creative potential, how each one wants to be in relationship, where each one wants to live... and so on.

In this way, a person learns to be in tune with his or her authentic inner reality, in which both the inner man and inner woman have enough space for their individual expression, which is bound to influence the choices a person takes in life. The inner has to find outer expression; the outer has to be in tune with the inner. This leads to wholeness and fulfillment.

Resonance is something that grows slowly in a person as his awareness and meditation grows; it cannot be expected to change during a single session. However, a therapist can make it clear what atmosphere and circumstances in life will be beneficial for a client's further development and what is likely to hinder it. So the person can create a lifestyle and personal environment that will be nourishing for his being, as he begins listening more to the neglected side of his inner polarity.

General Evaluation

Perhaps no other approach to therapy gives such importance to the art of meditative awareness, even creating a special tool for accessing this space and making it part of the therapeutic process. The resonance reading is an objective tool for measuring an inner state of consciousness, which makes it possible to adjust therapy work accordingly. It helps the therapist to understand the different potential of clients coming from different backgrounds, so each client is dealt with according to his needs and capacities. Moreover, the danger of over-estimating or under-estimating a client is reduced and this avoids any subtle pressure or expectation from the side of the therapist.

This approach to energy work is not goal-oriented, but is concerned with the present moment, here and now. A client does not take a series of sessions, as he may in Pulsation work; a single session is usually sufficient to get a clear perception of oneself right now.

Spiritual growth is understood as something that happens through relaxation and watchfulness, not through making an effort to achieve some future goal or ideal. Therefore this approach is contrary to most people's attitudes towards life, which are usually dominated by effort, purpose and ambition. For this reason, this type of work is effective in uprooting the foundation of the ego structure and allowing a deeper state of being to manifest in one's life.

To summarize: compared to other therapies this work focuses more on nourishing that which is already healthy, rather than struggling with tensions. This is based in trust that when the ego structure is deprived of support, it begins to dissolve by itself. The work gives practical insights into dealing with daily life in a way that is more in tune with the nature of the inner male and female energies.

Potential Pitfalls

I want to mention some points that can be counter-productive.

A system that includes psychic reading can give the impression to a therapist that one has now seen the whole truth and structure of a client's personality, even though it may be only a single aspect. The danger for an inexperienced therapist would be to adopt the position of one who can 'see all' and 'know all' about a client through such readings, rather than simply accompanying him through a process and allowing understanding to grow step by step. The beauty and depth of any session is to retain an element of mystery and surprise.

Also the concept of 'resonance' can be taken as a kind of scoring system, whereby it is seen as desirable to have a higher degree of resonance. It needs to be remembered that this is a tool to help the therapist respond to the client more accurately; the client should never be told about his level of resonance' because almost invariably it will be received as a judgment or criticism.

As a consequence, the ego is likely to enter from the back door, manifesting as a spiritual desire to be *more* developed and *more* aware. This danger is always present in models and systems in which clients are categorized and presented with a certain idea of what spiritual health means.

One more thing: there are many forms of energy work, including approaches that work exclusively with energy, with no psychological dimension, while others simply offer information – such as reading the content and condition of the chakras – with no deeper understanding of how healing or transformation occur. This chapter is not meant to be exhaustive, but presents an example of how such an approach can work as a form of therapy and counseling.

The uniqueness of this approach is that it does not simply pass on information, but shows clearly what information is beneficial to the client and his further growth.

Example of a Star Sapphire Session

The client, Rolf, is about 45 years old, in good health and has done a fair amount of meditation and other psychological and spiritual development work. He is aware of the concept of inner man and inner woman, but up to now has not had a session with this specific focus. He brings to the session the issue of being dissatisfied with his present work situation.

After an initial talk in which the therapist asks general questions about work, relationships and present spiritual practices, the therapist asks Rolf to lie down and then gives a reading to the client's left and right legs and to all the chakras. He finds a high general resonance, medium resonance in the right leg, some resonance in the left leg and resonance in various chakras.

Rolf's inner woman is an 'esoteric' type and not very grounded in practical things of life, while his inner man is more intellectual, enjoys writing and knows how to make it in the world. However, the man has a tendency to overestimate himself and become arrogant and judgmental towards the woman. The inner woman appears a bit sad and unsatisfied, as she didn't have much space to explore her own desires and likings. The man, on the other hand is tired, as it seems he has been carrying responsibility for both of them for quite a while.

Since this is clearly a type four session and Rolf has a good connection to his inner being, the therapist decides to address the issue directly and talk about some of his impressions gained during the energy reading. His intention is to confront the inner man, who takes too much space in Rolf's life, which in turn does not allow the inner woman to grow. At present, she does not have the strength to assert herself and take responsibility on her own. Consequently, the work in this session is to support and give more space to the inner woman, while confronting the inner man, who seems to think too much of his professional self-importance, while in reality he needs to rest, allowing space for 'less important' activities.

The therapist mentions to Rolf that his inner man is tired, almost exhausted, with the feeling that he has somehow been carrying the full weight of Rolf's working life for many years. In marked contrast, Rolf's inner woman has not been doing anything — is not, in fact, in touch with "the ground of ordinary daily life" at all — but lives in an ivory tower, far from reality.

In response to hearing this, Rolf agrees that his male side is tired and equates this with working for many years as the editor of a spiritual magazine, with little or no holidays. He comments that he has been thinking about changing his job to something less arduous, and the therapist points out that there will be a double benefit if he does so:

1. *His inner man will feel less burdened and will have more time to rest.*

2. *His inner woman can be invited to be more present in his actual*

life and develop her own creativity and interests, since it is clear that she enjoys those rare moments when Rolf is doing nothing.

As a result of the Gestalt work that follows, Rolf becomes enthusiastic about the insights the session is giving him. He likes the idea of inviting his inner woman to be more present in his life, and wants to explore how this can be done. At the same time, as a pragmatic man with specialized working skills, he will begin to look for a new kind of employment that will give him more free time and more opportunity to rest and relax.

At a follow-up session, several months later, Rolf reports that he has succeeded in obtaining a writing job which demands no more than three hours' work a day, giving him plenty of opportunity to explore the unfamiliar world of leisure. He discovers that his inner woman enjoys spending time in coffee shops, chatting with other women, and makes this a daily practice.

This new development also pleases his inner man, since this kind of social inter-action with women can also be used as an opportunity to flirt — something his inner man enjoys in a playful way.

Chapter Sixteen

Systemic Approaches

In a systemic approach to therapy the individual is not considered in isolation but in the context of a larger group; his behavior is understood in relation to other people, most notably the members of his original family: his father and mother, grandparents and siblings. In other words, the individual is seen as part of a family system that functions as an organic unity, where changes in the behavior of one family member will have an effect on all other members.

The most recent and widely known approach to systemic therapy is Family Constellation, developed by Bert Hellinger, a German therapist. In his method, a client selects individuals from a group of people – who may be known to him, or who may be strangers — to represent his family members, including one to represent himself. Without giving any explanation or instruction, the client positions these people to 'stand in' for original family members by placing them, without any gestures, in any way that he feels, in some kind of constellation.

What then becomes manifest is a significant and relevant portrait of the client's family: a configuration that expresses something about the degree of intimacy, pain, love, or sense of abandonment that each family member feels in relation to the others.

Under the guidance of a trained therapist, the stand-ins change position during the course of a session and are given brief sentences to say, usually simple one-liners, which reveal deep truths about the relationships between the family members whom they are representing. As the process unfolds they find different positions in relation to each other where, ultimately, everyone feels more at ease. The client remains a passive observer for most of the session, but towards the end usually gets positioned within the constellation, replacing the person who was representing him.

Whether or not the client participates, the overwhelming conclusion from such sessions is that the client experiences new insights into problems or tensions regarding his family and also a deep sense of relief.

This is the original style of Family Constellation, in which the therapist re-arranges the representatives and suggests sentences. But this work continues to develop and change; now, in many cases, therapists invite clients to create constellations in which fewer representatives are placed. These representatives are asked to observe and follow their spontaneous impulses and move accordingly without any talking. Consequently, the therapist becomes less active and more emphasis is given to the spontaneous feelings of the representatives and their non-verbal interaction.

A Mysterious Field of Energy

Behind the dynamics of Family Constellation is an invisible field of energy, in which participants in the process are able to access feelings and perceptions of the people they represent – people about whom they know very little and have never met. It is like stepping into the energy field of a family system and instantly being able to perceive certain truths about the relations within that system. This phenomenon is known by different commentators as a 'morphogenetic field,' an 'informing field,' or a 'knowing field.'

Hellinger himself sometimes places only one representative and then watches his spontaneous movements, perhaps adding another person later on. The movements, which can be very subtle and may become visible only after a long period, are termed by Hellinger 'movements of the soul' and 'movements of the spirit.'

This points to an understanding that these movements can bring to light the way each individual is influenced by a collective and connected to a universal force that is beyond his personal liking or disliking.

Without discussing all the implications of this style of work, one can see that Family Constellation has clearly moved from being an effective therapeutic technique towards something that is more similar to a meditation, where, through being a witness to the process, a person comes in touch with some deeper part of his being, or with an inner movement that is beyond his ordinary consciousness.

Even though these two approaches to Family Constellation sometimes seem to have nothing in common, both styles are connected to the same basic understanding of how a family system functions. In the 'old' way, all family members are present; it is clear who represents whom and important facts from the past of the family are explicitly included in the work. In the 'new' way, the energy field of the whole family is considered to be present, but things are deliberately kept more vague, leaving space for the 'soul' to receive what is necessary for healing.

Hidden Force of Collective Conscience

As we have already noted in preceding chapters, family conditioning happens to every child and is part of the process of developing a personal conscience. Because of the biological bond of a child to his mother, he assimilates not only what is important to his survival, but also the full range of her values and beliefs, which then become part of his own personal conscience.

Family Constellation has discovered that, in addition to personal conscience, there is a collective or family conscience that is very powerful and works equally on every member of a family system. Suffering occurs when an individual wishes to follow his personal conscience and when this personal desire comes into conflict with the collective law.

For example, a child sees his mother in pain, which is difficult for him to tolerate because he is so closely bonded to her. Because of this bond, he has the urge to do something for this person, who has done so much for him; he wants to 'return' something to her, or at least relieve her pain in some way. In this way, he starts imagining that through his own suffering, he can relieve his parent of suffering, which is existentially impossible.

For example, if the mother suffered a deep loss, such as the death of a dear sister, or of an earlier baby, then her own child may unconsciously choose to be sad and suffer in the magical belief that this will somehow ease the burden of his mother. In Family Constellation, this kind of love by a child for his mother is called 'blind' because it does not acknowledge the reality that no one else can carry a person's feelings and life destiny.

Even in adult relationships it is difficult to remain in a joyful mood when a loved one goes through a painful experience, so one can imagine how much more difficult it must be for a young child trying to cope with the suffering of a mother or father. Inevitably, to remain joyful would cause a deep sense of guilt for this child and this is one of the main reasons why, even as adults, it is often easier to live a life of suffering than happiness and joy. Happiness is often accompanied by a feeling of guilt. Even though everyone says 'I want to be happy' the underlying reality is that many of us feel more comfortable with misery.

Recognizing a Sacred Order

One of the basic laws discovered by Family Constellation is that there is an unchangeable order within every family: those who have arrived earlier in a family have a certain priority over those who arrived later, and this gives everyone a unique place in the family structure that belongs only to him. No one else can stand in this particular place. A parent is a parent, simply because he came first, and a child is a child because he arrived later. By trying to 'help' or 'save' a parent from pain, the child tries to assume the position of being a parent to his parent, thereby reducing his own parent to a child. This violates the order and suffering is an inevitable consequence.

Another important law governing family systems is that everyone who belongs to a particular system has an equal right to be acknowledged. When one family member is forgotten or condemned, this law is violated and the 'forgotten' or 'rejected' person will have to be represented by another member of the family – often, by a child of a later generation. In this way, the collective conscience is trying to bring this person back and give him his 'right' to be seen and acknowledged.

There are many reasons why family members are rejected or deliberately 'forgotten': someone went mad, or killed his wife, or became an alcoholic, or somehow disgraced the family, or disappeared to another country and never returned…or simply died early in life. But according to the law of belonging, all of these people need to be acknowledged and this means that if a person from an earlier generation is forgotten, or somehow denied, then he or she is bound to be represented by a later member of the family.

Under the influence of this force, a child can carry the forgotten person's feelings and attitudes without ever having met that family member personally. This is the main reason for what is called 'trans-generational entanglements,' which is a very important and surprising discovery of the Family Constellation method.

On an individual level, we are familiar with the principle that whatever we reject does not disappear but remains as a powerful force and govern our behavior from the unconscious part of the mind. In Family Constellation, a similar principle can be observed at an unconscious collective level over generations: the importance of rejected and forgotten family members.

People who are not family relatives can also belong to a system. For example, when a person in the past has been killed or violated in some way, and a family member was either the victim or the perpetrator, then either the victim or the perpetrator will be represented by someone from a later generation, depending on who has been rejected or forgotten.

In this way, Family Constellation shows how judgments and opinions about past family members lead to entanglements beyond the control of the individual. The moment we adopt an attitude of 'better' or 'worse' towards anyone from the family system, or if we think 'this should not have happened,' we violate the collective law that everyone has an equal right to be acknowledged and that we have no right to hold judgmental opinions about what happened in the past.

The Personality Model

In this approach to therapy, inter-personal relations between people are seen as following a principle that seeks to create a balance between giving and receiving. On a personal level, if something has been received from someone, there is a deep need to return something of equal value. On a collective level, there is a force that wants to balance whatever happened to someone, rather like a thermostat seeking equilibrium.

However, relationships between adult partners and relationships between parents and children are significantly different. Between men and women, there is a possibility to achieve a certain balance between what one partner gives to the other and what he receives from the other. If this balance is not respected, then eventually the relationship is disturbed, or will break up, because the underlying imbalance creates a sense of inequality between the partners.

Between parents and children no such balance is possible, because what a child receives from his parents is so much more than he ever will be able to return. The very nature of the relationship is one of imbalance, which ultimately leads to the separation of a child from his parents, which in fact is a healthy movement. One way to arrive at some kind of balance is for the child, now an adult himself, to give to his own children and in this way the need for balance can be seen as a force that sustains the continuing survival of the family and the collective group.

Family Constellation says that a child, in relation to his parents, is existentially 'small' and will always be in the receiving position. In relation to his own child, he is existentially 'big' and in the giving position. But in relation to an adult love partner a person is neither 'big,' nor 'small,' he is an 'equal,' if the relationship is healthy, because they both give and receive in a balanced way.

In brief, this is the personality model to which Family Constellation refers. One part of the personality is like a needy child, while another part is strong enough to give unconditionally. There is another part that is also in need, but this is not the need of a child who expects to be loved unconditionally; it is the need of an adult, who is aware of his own incompleteness. So this part of the personality needs, and is able to give and share, at the same time.

Looking at this model, it is easy to understand how interpersonal problems arise. For example, when a mother feels the need to be loved and appreciated by her own child, then psychologically she is not really relating to her child, but to her parents. When a child judges his parents or wants to give emotional support to them, he is trying to act as a parent to them. In a relationship between two adults, one partner may demand unconditional love and therefore remain identified with the role of the child, while the other, when tolerating this behavior, is choosing to remain in the role of the parent.

In relationship counseling, Family Constellation contributes to finding the real source of a problem by creating awareness about whether one's behavior is in tune with the nature of a balanced adult relationship. If not, then the problem may be found in an unnatural relation to one of the parents.

For example, rather than focusing on improving communication with a love partner, a client may realize that he is adopting the role of a needy child who is expecting unconditional love, and in this way he may be able to see that the real problem lies in his relationship with his parents. From this starting point, using the systemic approach, the client may discover, for example, that his mother lost one of her parents early in life and was unable to receive love; unconsciously, he has been trying to replace her parent, acting more as her parent than her child and therefore remaining unfulfilled himself.

Untangling the Family Knot

The client may come to see that his problem, or issue, has nothing to do with his current relationship with an adult love partner. These kinds of problems and entanglements are very common in adult relationships and Family Constellation is an effective way of untangling the knot.

Untangling happens in different ways. One important step is to discover who has been excluded from a family system and is therefore not represented and remembered with love. Bringing this person into the picture of the constellation and into a client's conscious awareness usually results in a sense of relief and inner expansion. It is similar to the sense of self-love and self-acceptance we can experience when we recognize and include some quality in us that we have been rejecting.

A Family Constellation facilitator will pay attention to any family member who has no proper place within the system, and will help a client look at this person with a new sense of love and respect. This can be difficult at times, especially if this excluded person happens to be the perpetrator of a crime.

Respect, in this form of therapy, does not only mean coming closer to someone; it can also mean allowing this person to follow his own destiny and accepting a necessary separation. As far as creating suffering is concerned, clinging to someone is as big a factor as rejection.

Ultimately, it is all about rising to a state of consciousness where one can experience love as respect and gratitude rather than as emotion. For example, when it is found that a client carries a pain for his mother, it is necessary for him to learn to respect her suffering without interference from his side. This is also a way of respecting the 'order' or nature of their relationship, whereby he is only a child and should be in a position of receiving rather than giving, bringing awareness to what it means for a child to love his parents.

Many times in Family Constellation sessions it becomes clear that the mother does not want her child to suffer on her behalf, and this helps to create the right understanding in the client and enable him to let go of a 'blind' desire. In fact, seeing her child happy and fulfilled usually contributes far more to a mother's joy than if the child tries to relieve her pain.

In 'blind' love, one is only aware of oneself and one's own desire, while 'conscious' love is also able understand the wishes of others. This points to another helpful aspect of Family Constellation: one can directly see the feelings and life circumstances of other family members and learn to comprehend them more deeply. Our hearts open when we understand that no one can be judged, because everyone is part of a bigger collective in which there is no 'bad' person — all are considered equal.

Uniqueness of Family Constellation

The basic points of systemic therapy in short:

1. Seeing everyone as part of a collective, not just as individuals, can make it easier to understand and love others, as well as ourselves. A client is influenced by and belongs to a collective field that includes not only his own family, but also his nation, race and ethnic group, all of which influence him in ways that are beyond his ideas and personal wishes.

2. The work is practical and down-to-earth, bringing the client in direct contact with his biological roots and his natural place in his family system. We come into this world through our parents, so our connection to them is very important, and this is the reason why therapy tries to heal any dysfunction in this foundational relationship. Facing one's own mother or father in a systemic constellation immediately connects a person to a deep inner movement that reveals significant truths about the client. It is also a practical and effective test to see where a person's personal development has reached.

3. Family Constellation can be seen in two ways: as an effective therapy and as a meditation. As a therapy it is a short-term approach that has a strong effect even after a single session and for this reason it is not recommended to do a 'series' of sessions, because one does not 'work through' an issue in the usual methodical way. As a meditation, it brings a client in contact with his ability to watch and say 'yes' to his inner state, without trying to interfere or change anything. In Family Constellation one learns to acknowledge what is and give up the desire to be someone else, and this includes accepting and loving one's parents as they are, which is the shortest way to find inner strength and peace. The ultimate expression of meditation is a pure state of consciousness that is free of all ties and conditioning, so it may seem strange to respect a family hierarchy. But, paradoxically, by acknowledging the ways in which we are tied to the past, transcendence becomes possible.

4. Family Constellation is simple and solution-oriented. There is no lengthy analysis. The therapist focuses on what moves the energy of the client and strengthens him. Many clients are used to 'talking about' their problems and enjoy reiterating them to anyone who will listen, which is a classic way of preventing real change to occur, but with this approach the essential is usually

clear after a short while and also revealed in the energy field. So there is no long talk with a client at the beginning of a session, as is sometimes the case in ordinary counseling.

5. Family Constellation can be a good way to bypass, what is called 'resistance' in a client, because the therapist does not work directly with the client himself. Instead, he works with the representatives in the constellation, leaving the client as a passive observer who is free to take in whatever he is ready to receive and leave whatever he cannot yet absorb. The client's freedom and dignity remains intact and the situation is avoided in which the therapist 'knows' and the client is 'ignorant.'

6. Family Constellation has found important connections between certain somatic and psychosomatic illnesses and the family dynamics that can lead to them. In this way, it is a great contribution in the healing and understanding of common problems like cancer, bulimia, depression, schizophrenia, addiction, neurodermatitis, to name just a few.

Areas for Improvement
Looking at the downside, there are a few points that need more attention:

1. In Family Constellation, the physical dimension is not included. One's psyche may understand a certain entanglement issue, but the body still carries the old pattern and any blocked energy may remain repressed. So the physiology of the body needs to be included as part of a comprehensive approach, for example, through using active and expressive methods like Osho's Dynamic Meditation, because one cannot let go of an energy before owning and experiencing it.

2. There are certain issues that may require a therapist to

accompany a client for a longer period than a single session. For example, when dealing with issues of trauma, a client may need support to develop a stronger physical container. Also, it may be necessary to prepare a client to absorb what a constellation brings to light and also to help him integrate it. So the attitude of doing a single constellation and then leaving things to the client may be inappropriate for some clients. A therapist needs to observe a delicate balance: to support a client without taking over his responsibility; to allow him to deal with his life by himself without overlooking his need for help.

3. Some practitioners of this method have developed a tendency to draw conclusions based on acquired knowledge rather than on direct observation. This is the danger when an approach offers a simple comprehension of complex problems and a practitioner tries to fit the issue into a certain category. In such cases, the energy of the constellation is not respected and the client is not benefited.

Example of a Family Constellation Session

Yuri is a client from Hungary, a country that was ruled for decades by a Communist regime. Since separating from his wife a year ago, his young daughter's epilepsy has worsened and this is his main motivation for requesting a session. During the interview, he cannot state any major reason for the separation. Inquiring about family history, it is found that he comes from an anti-communist background: his grandfather had once been sentenced to death for conspiracy by the communist regime. The sentence was not carried out, but he was forced to live outside the city, apart from his family. Yuri's wife, in marked contrast, comes from a pro-communist background and her grandfather was a well-known leader of the communist party.

When asked to place representatives for himself, his wife and his daughter in a constellation, Yuri places them so that neither parent is looking at their child. His own representative looks far into the distance, while his wife's representative looks at the floor. The child raises her arms as if she wants to protect someone, which seems to be her father.

From this constellation picture the therapist assumes that there are people missing in the picture. He also knows that, in Family Constellation, a person looking at the ground is actually looking at one or more people who have died. Based on information from Yuri's initial interview he forms a certain hypothesis: the wife, who looks to the ground, is looking at the victims of the communist party, while Yuri, looking far away, is looking at the communist leaders.

This hypothesis is based on the understanding that whoever is not honored and respected in a system is bound to be represented by a later child. In Yuri's family, the communists are excluded, and in his wife's family it is the anti-communists. This hypothesis will need to be verified through introducing the missing persons and noting their impact on the representatives already in the constellation.

The therapist introduces three stand-ins representing communist party leaders, who are placed in front of Yuri, and three for victims of the communist party, whom he places lying down on the floor where Yuri's wife is looking. Immediately, the wife starts moving towards the victims, while Yuri is staring intently at the party leaders.

From this point in the session, time and space are given for the energy to build and for deeper movements to develop. The therapist does not interfere and no one speaks, but it is apparent that the representatives are being steadily more affected by their roles.

The wife eventually lies down next to the victims. Yuri begins to make sounds, then screams, then lies on the floor and turns and twists in seeming agony, or cramps, replicating an epileptic fit.

To the therapist, it becomes clear that the daughter is carrying a burden for her father. In fact, it is really her father who is epileptic – she has relieved him of his destiny, taking on his suffering. This development also shows that the epilepsy is a held-back aggressive impulse; it is not Yuri's aggression, but the aggression that the client's family could not express against the communists. It is also the aggression that the communists exerted upon Yuri's family and in particular on his grandfather.

Ultimately, the possibility of healing in this family system manifests when the two sides meet and acknowledge all those who lost their lives and suffered. At the same time, Yuri and his wife accept that they need to leave their family members to their own destinies and slowly withdraw themselves from those who preceded them.

Healing is achieved when a person is placed to represent the whole country, thus making it clear that they are all deeply connected with each other. All representatives, including communists and anti-communists, bow with respect to the representative of the country and only after this has happened can Yuri and his wife look at each other and acknowledge that they have been identified with people on opposite sides of the political fence, and therefore their marriage was bound to fail.

Now they can also look at their child, who bursts in tears as she feels relieved of the pain she has been carrying. The parents hold their child in their arms and the love between the three becomes visible. We see here how a larger conflict, one that involves a whole nation, is being played out within the smaller unit of a single family, and no one is to blame for the fact that the relationship ended.

It is clear that the daughter's sickness results from her unconscious desire to take over the destiny of her father and his family. The sickness became more acute at the time of the separation of Yuri and his wife, because when they parted the child stayed with her mother; this made the child wish to take on even more of her father's pain as a way to compensate for the fact that he was the one who stayed alone. Children always try to keep a connection with both parents and they make an effort to create some kind of balance if they perceive one parent as less fortunate.

At the end of the session, Yuri understands his entanglement with his family's past struggle against the communist party and he is clear that he needs to allow some distance from them. At the same time, he needs to take personal responsibility as a father and in this way protect his daughter, rather than allowing her to try and protect him. Therefore, the therapist asks Yuri to explain to his daughter that he wants her to stay with her mother, as this is the safer place for her.

Chapter Seventeen

Working with Groups

This last chapter gives hints to therapists who are leading courses for groups of people, or who are planning to do so. Leading a group follows the same basic principles as giving individual sessions; the main difference is that a facilitator needs to be able to hold the attention of many people, guide them collectively and deal with the bigger energy that they generate. Not surprisingly, most therapists like to gain experience in individual work before leading groups.

The work goes through similar phases. As with individual therapy, a facilitator builds trust in the first phase, explores the depth of the topic in the second stage and allows time for integration in the third and final phase.

Phases of a Group Process

It would be a misunderstanding to suppose that the main function of a group facilitator is to give instructions for participants to follow. He is more like a coordinator, who makes sure that certain rules are being observed and guides people towards certain experiences.

In order to do this, the rules of a particular course need to be made clear in the beginning and there needs to be an agreement among all participants that they are willing to play in the same ballpark, so to speak.

Once they are in agreement, it will help to create trust if they know that the therapist is ready, willing and able to ensure that everyone follows the rules. This will create a safe field for everyone and help them relax. The most important rule in a group process is that everyone has the same right to speak and express himself, and the emphasis of expression needs to be on talking about oneself, not commenting on others, or judging others for what they expose or reveal about themselves.

In order to build the energy of a group and take people deeply into a process where personal issues can be addressed, it is advisable to deal with 'problematic' clients – those who cannot easily fall in tune with the process — later in the workshop, giving more space in the beginning to those who have no problem participating in the work.

This mirrors the process that happens in individual therapy where a counselor first supports presence and only afterwards moves towards the roots of the client's ego-structure. Similarly, in a group process, participants with more presence can help the course leader, especially in the beginning, to validate the process and build a solid ground for everyone else to follow. Once this has been accomplished, it will be easier for the course leader to deal with clients with less presence more effectively and without unsettling the whole group.

The same principle can be remembered when people ask questions, or when there is a 'group sharing' in which participants are invited to express whatever they are experiencing. It is not necessarily the case that those who want to do most of the talking have the most to contribute — we will return to this point later.

After the initial phase has been completed, sensitive issues can be explored more deeply and more challenging structures can be used that may provoke uncomfortable or disturbing feelings in some participants.

In the last and final phase, there should be enough time for participants to integrate and absorb insights from the process without being confronted with new material. As with individual sessions, it is important that participants leave a group process in a grounded way, not overwhelmed by what they have experienced, either positively or negatively.

Naturally, there will be differences between members of a group, for example, how much they can handle, and this will also affect how quickly or slowly the process proceeds — according to their capacity. A good course leader will be able to balance the process for those who participate easily and for those who find it difficult.

Setting Up a Workshop Space

Every course has to adjust to the facilities in which it is held, but there are variables that can be changed according to the kind of psychological atmosphere a facilitator chooses to create. Small details of how a room is prepared for a course can help to create a supportive energy field or a more challenging one. It can help people feel safe and relaxed, or perhaps more insecure and uncertain, or inspire them to become creative.

Some possible set ups:

A course room can be set up with chairs, or cushions, for participants to sit on and these can be arranged in different ways that will create different moods. For example, they can be arranged in a circle, with the course leader as part of the circle, or facing the front in a way that sets the course leader apart, as the 'leader,' and participants become an audience. A third option is to invite participants into a room that has not been previously set up and ask them to find their own place. They can also be invited to either sit or stand.

When everyone sits in a circle, it is more likely that a feeling will be created of doing something together, and when the facilitator sits in front, some participants are likely to project an authority figure onto him. Either structure can be useful, depending on what the facilitator wants to achieve.

When a room is prepared in the same way every day, according to a fixed pattern,, participants may feel more secure, knowing where to sit and probably finding a 'favorite' spot that becomes their temporary home. The downside of this strategy reflects the fact that people tend to behave habitually and so, after a few days, they may begin to think and act in a mechanical way.

With a more open set up, where no seats are positioned in advance, participants will need to make their own choices, deciding where to sit, or what to do, and this will require them to check-in with themselves about how they feel in the moment. This is more challenging and creative, but may also create insecurity in some participants.

Much depends on the intention of the therapist, or facilitator. Generally speaking, after an initial phase, it may help to surprise people, so they are challenged to be more alert and provoked to stay away from routine behavior patterns.

The Facilitator

The inner attitude of a therapist who is facilitating a group is similar to one who is conducting an individual session. It is important that the facilitator trusts and follows his own rhythm, making his own decisions about when to say, or do something. Timing and the respect for gaps, silences and waiting are also essential for helping the collective group energy to settle and gain depth.

In an individual session, the therapist takes care that no aspect of the client's energy is denied or rejected; similarly, in a group, he takes care that no member of the group is excluded or feels rejected. Often, it is the outsiders who have the most potential and the group leader needs to connect with them and let them know – not necessarily with words – that they are included in the process.

In general, the work is to support responsibility in participants rather than training them to follow a structure. For example, sometimes participants do not feel capable, or are not willing, to join an exercise or structure and in such cases it is usually better not to insist that they should join, but rather allow them to remain resting and observing. They can be included again at a later moment, perhaps by asking how they are feeling.

It is better to allow people to make their own choices rather than insisting that they should participate in all structures. At the most one can help someone understand the meaning and purpose of a group structure or exercise as a way of inviting them to participate.

Throughout the course there needs to be a subtle balance between structured sessions and more open sessions where participants have the possibility to follow their own impulses and digest any experience from a previous exercise.

If a therapist shows that he trusts the participants, they will respond by trusting the therapist and the process. Trying to overly control what participants do exposes the insecurity of a therapist and the participants will respond by becoming more afraid themselves.

Moments in which a therapist does not know what to do next — and the ability to allow such moments — is an important ingredient in any group process. A group where everything is pre-planned with a fixed sequence of structures lacks moments of surprise and spontaneity that give a group process depth and significance. A therapist's ability to wait, not knowing what to do next, and his courage to act without hesitation when needed, will encourage a balance between alertness and relaxation in the participants.

Structure Versus Freedom

Generally speaking, there should be more structures at the beginning of a course, with clear instructions what to do. This will help the participants feel safe and settled. Later in the process, when participants are more at ease and more in contact with themselves, a therapist can introduce more choices and freedom of response, thereby enhancing self-responsibility.

For example, in the beginning, while leading a guided

meditation, a course leader may instruct people with specific guidelines — whether they should stand, sit or lie down, if they should close their eyes, if they should sit up straight and so on. Later, he may give alternatives, such as "choose between standing or sitting" and again later in the course he may even drop that and say "allow your body to find the position it wants to be in right now." If he had said this at the beginning, some people may have felt lost, not knowing what to do, or acting out of habit without being able to tune in and feel what the body really wants to do. This is a simple example of how introducing more flexibility, freedom of choice and selfresponsibility is a step-by-step process.

It is, of course, important to take note of what type of participants are in a particular course. If participants are mature and experienced in meditation, they can be given more freedom and responsibility from the beginning, and they can also take part in choosing the direction of a course. Otherwise, they may feel bored, resistant or simply unwilling to join an exercise. A course filled with beginners will need clear direction and instructions. Such participants may not be able to benefit from an instruction that says "follow your feeling;" they may not know how to answer, when asked what they would like to do next.

The depth of a course depends on the level of presence of the participants and the therapist. The more presence, the deeper it will go. A group that consists only of structures and guided exercises cannot lead to much presence or depth, as these qualities are the consequence of meeting people individually, in their essence. So the course leader's abilities and clarity in individual work with people will determine how deep a group process can be. A person, who is not skilled in individual and personal work cannot lead a course that has depth and profundity.

Individual work in a group can happen as part of a general sharing, or as a demonstration session during the course, conducted in the middle of the group, where a particular method is shown to people, or a specific topic is explored more deeply. Working with one participant will affect others and is important for almost everyone.

Inspiring Others

In order to inspire others, a therapist or facilitator needs to feel inspired himself, sharing his own understanding and enthusiasm. So a group leader should take care that he enjoys what he is doing, even in small details. This may include taking care that he is not bored with his own music, or with the exercises he is using, or with the theoretical material he presents.

However, enthusiasm is a double-edged sword. A charismatic leader can easily overpower people with his energy and spirit, and this is likely to turn participants into admirers and followers rather than helping them to focus on themselves and their growth. A methodical leader may not be so inspiring, but he is more likely to pace his students and choose methods that are best for them, rather than displaying his own powers.

A good therapist is one who is not really a leader. He accompanies his students, neither pulling them ahead nor pushing them from behind. He is more a friend than a guide and shares his experience when relevant, without talking too much about himself.

Group Sharing

'Sharing' is a common term given to a specific time in a course when participants are invited to communicate their personal experience to the whole group, to ask questions or to express themselves in some other way. This type of structure can give the course leader important feedback about the energy of the whole group, so that he can decide how best to proceed. It also offers an opportunity to include participants who feel lost or who are not fully participating in the process.

The therapist does not have to respond in the same way to each participant who speaks. He may respond to some participants quite simply, to others more profoundly, and he can also use part of the time to work with an individual in more depth on a certain topic. Usually, he will choose a participant and topic according to what he considers to be most beneficial for everyone to watch.

As mentioned at the beginning of this chapter, every participant has an equal right to express himself, but in most circumstances he should not be allowed to comment on other people's experience. At most, he can say, "What 'X' has just shared touches me…" and then continue with his own experience.

Often, in a sharing, some participants tend to speak more frequently and longer, while others remain more silent. This does not mean that those who are eager to talk have more to contribute; on the contrary, it is sometimes the 'quiet ones,' who have meaningful insights to share. Knowing this, the group leader can invite silent participants to express themselves, especially if he feels they have something valuable to contribute.

However, this strategy has its downside, because in a way the therapist is taking responsibility for those participants and interfering in the natural flow of events. Much depends on the intuition of the therapist, who must balance encouragement of expression with the need to leave responsibility for sharing with the participants. He should not assume the role of a guide or parent, but accept the fact that not everyone needs to express himself in every group sharing.

If a therapist opens the space for a group sharing and nobody speaks, this can mean that, at this time, the participants do not have any need to express themselves verbally. It can also indicate that people are afraid and in this case the therapist needs to give more time, be more inviting, and perhaps lower the level of anxiety.

One way of preparing people for self-expression is to ask

participants to start by sharing in smaller groups, or with just one partner, before creating a sharing situation for the group as a whole.

Some participants are eager to receive gratification from the therapist, treating him as a parent, wanting his approval or attention, and this can be a strong motivation for sharing. It is important for a therapist to avoid slipping into such a role too frequently, and this can be achieved by bringing the strategy to the attention of the individual and to the group; perhaps exposing and acknowledging the underlying motivation rather than simply fulfilling a client's desire for approval.

The depth and quality of group sharing will naturally intensify as the course progresses. In the beginning, a therapist may be satisfied if participants simply report any experiences they are having as a result of the process, while later on he may invite people to look at more subtle psychological, emotional or energetic phenomena.

Questions and Answers

It can be helpful to create separate occasions for a question-and-answer session, rather than including it as part of a general sharing session, particularly in trainings where people are studying a method or technique and need to ask questions in order to understand a complex process.

Asking questions and receiving answers is an intellectual process. This may be necessary in order to deepen understanding, but it can also prevent a person from contacting a deeper space inside. For example, a participant may ask a series of questions simply to avoid connecting with his feelings, and a course leader can help such a person by inviting him to look at his motivation for asking. In this way, a client is helped to enter a process rather than staying on the periphery of it.

Supporting Individual Sharing

The way to support a participant's sharing is similar to individual counseling. Generally speaking, the therapist supports presence and either ignores or confronts the participant's mind and his desires. This will depend on a variety of factors: what kind of participant is sharing, what stage the group process has reached, how much time can be devoted to sharing, and so on.

Participants who are in contact with their inner being deserve more attention and energy than those who remain at an intellectual level. But everyone can be invited to connect with what they are experiencing in the present moment, regardless of their inner state, or the depth of the process. Those who start to talk about a previous experience can be guided away from long storytelling by asking them to focus on the relevance to what they are experiencing now.

If a person still does not wish to talk about himself after being invited to do so three times, a therapist should not insist further but continue to the next person. While listening to participants, a therapist should also observe their body language and general demeanor, as this may reveal a deeper truth than the words being said.

Naturally, some participants are better at expressing themselves than others and as a result may receive more attention in a group sharing, but the course facilitator should take care that everyone in a group feels included and no one feels left out. This is one of the basic functions of a coordinator of any group, whether in therapy or elsewhere: he takes care that everyone feels acknowledged equally in his right to be member of the group.

Dealing with Projections

Projection, which we discussed in chapter eight, is one of the main issues that arise in therapy and a group facilitator needs to understand this phenomenon and how to deal with it. Projection is magnified in a group process, not only by the fact that many people can be projecting at the same time, but also because clients tend to project more on a course facilitator than on an individual therapist.

Projection is a defense mechanism, whereby unwanted feelings, or feelings that one cannot access directly, are placed on another person, so that these feelings appear to be coming from that person. A projection can be negative or positive, but the solution is always the same: one has to start to looking at oneself rather than at the other person, discovering and owning the denied feeling within. For example, if one feels that others are not attentive or loving, then a good question to ask oneself is, "In what way am I not attentive or loving to myself?" or, "In what way am I not attentive and loving to others?"

If the projection is directed by one participant towards another, the therapist can point out the basic dynamic, even before dealing with the issue that has provoked it. If the projection is directed towards the therapist himself, then it is less easy, because the participant may react to any statement the therapist makes. In this case, it is better not to point out the dynamic, as the therapist's observation that "you are projecting on me" is unlikely to be accepted.

It is usually more productive for a therapist to fully allow the projection to happen, maybe even supporting it for a moment, so the participant has the space to discover his own energy behind it and perhaps eventually owning it as a part of himself.

However, as a first step, a therapist will have to note if any feelings have been triggered in himself, whether positive or negative, and whether the projection has been caused by some unconscious behavior from his side. If this is so, it is helpful to acknowledge this, sometimes even openly, rather than pretending to be aloof, centered and unaffected. Then he can begin to move out from his own reaction, becoming more present, because only from a state of presence will the therapist be able to help the participant come to a point where he can own his projection.

An effective method to do this is the Gestalt technique described in chapter six, where the client is asked to place two pillows opposite each other, one representing himself and the other representing the therapist. A dialog can begin between the two sides, where the client plays both persons alternately and the therapist remains an outsider. This makes it easier for the therapist to work with the client than if the energy remains directed at him in person. However, this can be successful, only if the therapist is not using this technique as a way to protect himself and is not having any reaction, for example, of fear, defensiveness or a desire to control.

The same method can be of help when a group participant is projecting on another participant, as the work happens only with one person and the other is relieved. In this way, the facilitator can avoid a complex situation in which one person's projection starts triggering another person's projection and people react in a chain, disturbing the group energy.

Dealing with Disturbances

There may be other disturbances in a group process. A participant may be negative or critical, or someone may continuously ask intellectual questions without entering a process of self-inquiry. It is important, especially in the beginning, that a course leader does not give this too much attention or make an effort to change people's behavior, as this may aggravate the situation further. Instead, by supporting and building positive group energy, negative behavior will lose energy and may disappear by itself. If it remains a disturbance, then one can work with such participants at a later moment, when the group is more settled. In this way, any draining of the group energy is avoided, which can easily happen when one gives too much attention to negativity.

When the moment is appropriate to deal with 'difficult' participants, the work is like in a one-to-one session: the therapist waits for a gap in the client's stream of thoughts and desires, which is bound to happen sooner or later. In this gap, the therapist acts, or says something, that is concerned with the dimension of being and then immediately rests again. In this way the mind is deprived of support and loses energy, which will eventually shift the client away from his negativity.

As in individual sessions, the concern of a group leader should be to remain at ease and resist the temptation to try and impose his authority or implement strict controls. The work consists in holding a space for the participants, which is different from our usual understanding of 'helping.' He takes care to be in touch with a feeling of relaxation and well-being.

Leading a Guided Meditation

In personal growth courses it is essential to be able to lead guided meditations that connect participants to their inner being. This will create an inner space to absorb any new experiences, or learning, and also prepares people to let go of old thought patterns and beliefs.

Before starting a guided meditation the course leader has to be clear about his intention and direction, be in touch with his own energy and be aware of the energy of the group participants. In this way he can, for example, decide whether the guided meditation should be focused on movement, or stillness, on the body, mind or heart.

An easy way to start a guided meditation is to follow one's own need in the moment, then watch how participants respond to the instructions and in this way gently adjust the direction in which the meditation continues. It is helpful to watch participants who are more in touch with their being and observe how they respond; this will give an indication to the course leader whether his guidance is in tune with the energy of the moment.

By focusing on those who do fall in tune rather than those who do not, a momentum is created that creates a strong positive pull, which eventually no one will be able to resist. In this way, participants with less maturity will benefit from those who are more in touch with themselves. No one is forced to follow or made feel guilty, but the positive energy itself has an influence.

Instructions for guided meditations need to be inviting and there should be enough pauses for people to take the time to connect with themselves.

Summary

A course that promotes personal growth has to create a loving atmosphere where the participants feel at ease, supported and relaxed, so they can learn from each other, with each other, and make new experiences. Awareness grows in an atmosphere of love. The function of the course leader is twofold: he is a coordinator, who makes sure a certain structure is followed, and he enhances and supports moments where love and awareness arise spontaneously, in a natural way.

In a training, in which people are supposed to learn a certain method, or technique, it is important to balance teaching and learning with time for integration, relaxation and enjoyment. Otherwise the tension of learning can become counterproductive: stress builds up and less is absorbed. In general, real learning is not intellectual, but always comes from personal experience.

Epilogue

There is an ancient Indian parable about five blind men who meet an elephant and try to figure out what it is. One touches an ivory tusk and says, "An elephant is hard and smooth like a stone." Another touches a leg and says, "No, an elephant is thick and tall like the trunk of a tree." A third touches an ear and says, "No, an elephant is flat and wide like the sail of a ship..." and so on.

Each of the five men has a valid experience, but in reality the elephant is all of these things and much more. Similarly, the spiritual approach to therapy embraces a wide variety of techniques but is more than just the sum of its different parts.

Different forms of therapy approach a client, or individual, from different angles and standpoints and are therefore both unique and limited. No single viewpoint can claim to depict the wholeness of man. Each approach has a slightly different vision of what is meant by physical, psychological or spiritual health, as can be seen in the three different styles of therapy described in this book:

- Pulsation focuses on the understanding that health happens as a direct result of restoring the body pulsation, or natural rhythm, where energy can move freely through the musculature of the body.
- Energy work covers a vast range of therapy and healing, but generally speaking it understands health as a growth in consciousness. When this principle is applied to our inner male and inner female polarities, health is seen as the point at which they become fully conscious and rooted in their aloneness. Paradoxically, this is also the moment at which they can fully meet and dissolve into each other.
- Family Constellation understands health as being in tune with the movements of the soul or spirit, as expressed and conveyed

to us through our family and parents. When we move with the spirit, we acknowledge everyone as he or she is, and we find ourselves in agreement with everything as it happens.

These approaches point to different aspects of the same basic truth. When comparing them in a logical and systematic way, they may appear to be both complementary and contradictory. For example, Pulsation promotes healing through the expression of repressed energy, such as the release of pent-up anger, while another form of therapy may see this as strengthening a person's identification with this emotion. Pulsation stresses the importance of giving a series of sessions and working through a client's issues, while Family Constellation favors bringing a person in touch with a certain truth in a single session. What seems true and relevant when seen through one pair of glasses may look like a mistake through another pair.

But this does not have to be a problem. Life is far too complex to be explained by a single system. People who are interested in working on themselves through therapy can explore and experience different approaches, accepting contradictions without trying to find common ground. Any attempt to create a single system that contains all other approaches, as, for example, Psychosynthesis has tried to do, may simply result in the loss of all uniqueness and significance.

Besides, everything depends on the needs of the individual client and on the particular stage of growth that he, or she, is currently passing through. What is useful today may not be needed tomorrow, and what seems irrelevant now may be of significance later. To be able to contain contradictions and let this create an inner movement towards personal growth is to be in tune with life, which is full of apparent contradictions and opposites.

This is one reason why this approach is called the 'Zen way,' because Zen is existential and not confined to linear thinking and logic. Zen teachings are not really teachings. The function of a Zen Master is not to explain a certain philosophy but to help his disciples move to a state beyond the ordinary mind, where immediate understanding occurs spontaneously.

In this sense, healing can happen at a level that is beyond our normal concepts about health. Rather, healing happens as part of the mystery of life, bringing a person to a deep state of 'yes,' acknowledging life as it is, experiencing a state of acceptance and transcendence. In other words, this kind of therapy is rooted in meditation, since it is the function of meditation to bring people closer to their inner being – a being which resides in a natural and permanent state of 'yes' towards life.

Another important aspect of spiritual therapy, or counseling, is that it prepares the ground for a more creative way of living, which is not oriented towards fixing specific problems, but towards growing beyond personal limitations and contributing to the creativity of life.

Finally, it needs to be recognized that this book contains an inherent paradox, because, in the manner of Zen, the real thing cannot be said explicitly, but only indicated indirectly. Zen itself is aware of this problem, as illustrated by the following anecdote:

A curious traveler happened to meet a Zen Master sitting on a beach by the sea, and approached him to ask, "What is meditation?"

The Zen Master looked into his eyes for a long time, saying nothing.

"I'm sorry," said the traveler, "I do not understand your silence, please give me a better explanation."

The Master did nothing for a while, then picked up a stick and wrote in the sand, 'Zen.'

"That still does not help me much," said the traveler. "Can you please expand your explanation?"

The Master again paused for a while, then wrote in huge letters across the beach, 'ZEN!'

"You are still not saying very much," commented the traveler.

"On the contrary, I have said far too much," responded the Master. *"More than this I cannot say, I have already gone too far."*

Bibliography

The Roots of Love: A Guide to Family Constellation by Svagito Liebermeister (Perfect Publishers 2006)

The Master's Touch, Psychic Massage by Sagarpriya (Sandvik Publishing, 1994)

Tantric Pulsation by Aneesha Dillon (Perfect Publishers, 2005)

Waking the Tiger: Healing Trauma by Peter Levine (North Atlantic Books 1997)

Acknowledging What Is. Conversations with Bert Hellinger (Zeig Tucker & Theissen, Inc. 1994))

Love's Hidden Symmetry. What Makes Love Work in Relationships by B. Hellinger, G.Weber , H.Beaumont (Zeig Tucker & Theissen, Inc. 1998)

To the Heart of the Matter. Brief Therapies. by Bert Hellinger (Carl-Auer-Systeme Verlag, Heidelberg, 2003)

The Great Pilgrimage by Osho (Rebel Publishing House, India)

Beyond Psychology by Osho (Tao Publishing Pvt. Ltd., India)

The Rebellious Spirit by Osho (Rebel Publishing House, India)

Satyam, Shivam, Sunderam by Osho (Tao Publishing Pvt. Ltd., India)

Meditation. The First and Last Freedom by Osho (St. Martin's Press, USA)

About the Author

Svagito R. Liebermeister was born in Germany in 1957, holds a degree in psychology from Munich University, and has over 25 years practical experience in working with people as a therapist. He has studied a wide range of therapeutic approaches, including Deep Tissue Bodywork, Neo-Reichian Energy Work (Pulsation), Psychic Massage, Star Sapphire Energy Work, Counseling and Family Constellation. In each of these methods he has been leading numerous training programs, starting more than 20 years ago.

Parallel to his interest in therapy, Svagito has been a disciple of the Indian mystic Osho since 1981 and has explored a wide range of meditation techniques. He is interested in combining therapy with meditation and has trained hundreds of practitioners worldwide in the art of working with people.

Svagito is currently the coordinator of the annual Therapist Training Program at the Osho Meditation Resort in Pune, India, one of the largest personal growth centers in the world. Every year, he travels extensively through Europe, Asia, Central America and other parts of the world, offering courses and training programs in over 15 different countries.

His first book, 'The Roots of Love, A Guide to Family Constellation' (2006) has been translated into eight languages.

For further information about Svagito's courses and trainings, or to order his books and DVDs:
www.family-constellation.net
For further information about Osho and his approach to meditation:
www.osho.com

B O O K S

O is a symbol of the world, of oneness and unity. In different cultures it also means the "eye", symbolizing knowledge and insight. We aim to publish books that are accessible, constructive and that challenge accepted opinion, both that of academia and the "moral majority".

Our books are available in all good English language bookstores worldwide. If you don't see the book on the shelves ask the bookstore to order it for you, quoting the ISBN number and title. Alternatively you can order online (all major online retail sites carry our titles) or contact the distributor in the relevant country, listed on the copyright page.

See our website www.o-books.net for a full list of over 400 titles, growing by 100 a year.

And tune in to myspiritradio.com for our book review radio show, hosted by June-Elleni Laine, where you can listen to the authors discussing their books.

mySpiritRadio